MISSIONS
OF
OLD TEXAS

MISSIONS
OF
OLD TEXAS

James Wakefield Burke

SOUTH BRUNSWICK AND NEW YORK:
A. S. BARNES & COMPANY
LONDON: THOMAS YOSELOFF LTD

Library of Congress Catalogue Card Number: 76–126943

A. S. Barnes and Co., Inc.
Cranbury, New Jersey 08512

Thomas Yoseloff Ltd
108 New Bond Street
London W1Y OQX, England

ISBN 0-498-07784-5

Printed in the United States of America

To

Terry Lyn Burke, my daughter

who is a student at Ursuline Academy

Contents

Acknowledgment

Photos of the Texas missions by courtesy of the
Texas Highway Department

MISSIONS
OF
OLD TEXAS

1
Texas and the Little Brothers

T HE story of the missions of Texas is inseparable from the early
history of Texas territory. The dedicated and simple-living friars
who came and established the missions in the land now encompassed by the state left their mark and influence indelibly impressed on all that is modern Texas. The extent of mission activity
in Texas has never been realized. Historians are just becoming
aware of how widely and how deeply the foundations of Christianity were laid by the devoted friars. When thinking of missions
in the New World, the mind is naturally drawn to California. It is
interesting to note that one hundred years before the first mission
was established in that balmy state Texas had over twenty active
missions, seven formal presidios, and one Spanish military outpost.
There are herein records of fifty and more missions having been
established in Texas territory by the indefatigable friars, while those
established in California never exceeded half that number.

The visitor to the old missions would do well to allow himself
to muse upon the benefits that have been conferred upon mankind
by the labors, sufferings, triumphs, and defeats of the padres during their all too brief sojourn in the Southwest. One may divine in
the missions—even in their ruins—and their history the wealth of
culture, art, refinement, menticulture, and acculturation brought to
the New World by those intrepid fathers. The archaeologist, the
anthropologist, and the serious investigator into the origins of the
numerous Indian tribes that roamed the vast expanse of present
Texas are beginning to realize how valuable and thorough is the
information gathered by the patient Franciscan friars concerning
the customs and habits, the religion and habitat, of the aboriginal
peoples now completely departed from the land. Though their work
was confined to only a few tribes, its pure and unselfish purpose

13

and beneficent results cannot be questioned, for this is attested to in the annals of those times.

That which promotes the progress of one portion of mankind works ultimately for the benefit of the entire race. Great and lasting benefits were bestowed upon the Indians; and thus, later, the fruits of these benisons were to be appreciated and utilized by the white settlers. Millions in the family of man have rejoiced over the bright career of the Franciscan fathers in Texas and mourned its fate; if it had survived, it would have elevated the Indian tribes and preserved them from dispersion by white invaders. Although the padres dominated the Texas scene for less than a century and a half, all persons with a faith in civil rights and a love for humanity must deplore the passing of the missions. Their spiritual power and influence prepared the way for a civilization which came later under American sovereignty.

Texas, her past filled with romance and glory, her present one of peace and plenty, and promise of even richer and greater glories (glories that might well awe the mind of man), must pay homage to those "Little Brothers." Today the dusty trails on which those saintly men, with their worldly possessions on their backs, plodded their way from Mexico seeking savage people to convert to Christianity, are multiple ribbons of shining concrete, linking towns, states, and counties. Yesterday these missionaries journeyed through burning hot and dusty deserts, barren rocky wastes, great areas whose rough open surface impeded these travelers' every step. They zigzagged through long stretches of thorny mesquite and prickly cactus. They climbed up rugged mountains and descended dangerous, precipitous slopes that lacerated and bruised their bodies. They endured famine and thirst. They dragged themselves along by sheer power of will and the grace of God, suffering agonies of flesh and of the spirit. They finally arrived at their destination, placing the cross of Christ and the royal standard of Spain on the soil of Texas.

They brought into Texas the horse, the cow, and other domesticated beasts; they brought the honey bee, and even the bluebonnet, which they culled from the hillsides of Jerusalem and planted with the missions on Texas soil. Early legend tells us that this grateful flower clung to historic ground, and covered the spots where the blood of heroes was shed. Later it was chosen as the Texas state flower. The padres bequeathed a most pleasant architecture; they gave their names to rivers and villages; they left a heritage without which the colonizers would not have been able to win Texas independence. They brought the cross, and with it a desire for one man to love his fellows without quailing at the color of his skin. When Texans shout "Remember the Alamo!" there is, darkly yet reverently, behind this cry a small prayer which, in truth, must say: "Remember the Little Brothers!"

2

The Patron Saint of Texas

THE early history of Texas is the saga of the Franciscan friars. Who were the Franciscans? To know this order of padres, one must learn something about their founder, Francis of Assisi. The story of Saint Francis of Assisi has much in common with that of Jesus Christ and of Saint Paul of Tarsus, the Apostle. All three, in their time, endured all the temptations inherent in the body of the human creature.

Assisi is a small village not far from Naples, in Umbria, central Italy. Here lived a rich clothier named Pietro di Bernardone, who married a noblewoman of means, Lady Pica. To them was born a son and they named him Francis. The parents lavished many riches upon their son, so that he grew up a fun-loving, spoiled youth who loved pretty girls, wine, and the gay life of the times. In our modern days he would have been called a "playboy." He was a daring and dauntless rider and a champion of jousting. His admiring friends acclaimed him king of the youth of Assisi. In that period it was the thing for sons of noble and rich families to become knights. This Francis aspired to do: he would be admired by everyone and would receive added adulation from his friends and the pretty girls he liked to court.

His parents, unable to deny their son anything, allowed him to become a knight; and in the year 1202 he and a group of his friends volunteered for service in a war between Assisi and Perugia. Francis was among those taken prisoner, and as months went by all the young captives, except Francis, became increasingly melancholy. Strangely, Francis became more cheerful; he devised endless games, spun verse and songs to sustain his companions. After almost a year in prison they were set free and returned to Assisi.

The city-states which made up Italy at that time constantly

16

feuded and warred with one another, and the next military venture was directed against the city-state of Sicily. Francis was chosen to lead the expedition. He set out on horseback at the head of his band of young warriors. When they had traveled some distance, Francis' horse suddenly balked and reared, its eyes rolled in its head, and, as if by an unseen giant hand, was snatched from beneath his rider. Francis lay in the dust senseless for a time. When he recovered he mounted his horse, bade his companions farewell, and turned back to Assisi.

He was not the same person. Francis himself, many years later, said that while he lay unconscious he was blessed by a revelation of his life's meaning, in much the same way as was Saint Paul after falling in the dust outside Jerusalem. A voice, he said, bade him repudiate war and turn back and serve the cause of peace.

Try as his father and mother did, they could not induce him to continue the old life of rich society. Alone and derided he wandered about at loose ends, trying to find himself. His father tried to turn him to work and industry by making him an assistant in his textile establishment. The youth was becoming increasingly sensitive to the harsh contrasts of the social order. While his family and his friends had an abundance of all the good things in life, there were others, the poor and inferior, who were constantly in dire want of the bare necessities of life. He went about talking and arguing for civil equalities for everyone. Because of his youthful zeal and in his concern for the deprived, he would give away clothes or money from his father's establishment.

One day Francis had another vision. A saint came to him and said: "Francis, repair my church which falleth into ruin." He had no money of his own, so he sold a large stock of his father's newly arrived cloth in order to raise money for rebuilding Saint Damian's Church which was falling into ruin. Angered, his father first kept him at home and later cited him before civil authorities. When Francis refused to answer the summons, his father called him before the Bishop. When the accusations were made, Francis without a word peeled off his garments and handed them to his father. "Until now I have called you my father on earth," he said. "Henceforth I can truly say: Our Father Who art in heaven." The astonished Bishop gave him a cloak, and Francis went out into the chilly air singing. Liberated at last from ties of social position and family and even such material possessions as clothing, he was elevated with spiritual bliss. Now, with nothing, he had come into his own.

He sought experiences to confirm him in his new life. He mingled with beggars and in rags begged alms. He sought out lepers, and to purge himself of his horror of them he kissed the hand of the first afflicted one he met; he spent much time comforting them and ministering to them. He repaired the Church of Saint Damian with his bare hands; he restored a chapel dedicated to Saint Peter the Apostle, and the now famous chapel of Saint Mary of the Angels, and the Portiuncula, on the plain below Assisi. Thus Francis proved to his own inner satisfaction that "he who loseth his life shall find it." He went about singing of his joy and fulfillment. He was one with the universe.

Although a layman, Francis began to preach to the townspeople. Disciples joined him, and for them he composed a simple rule of life. Francis' rule was "To follow the teachings of our Lord Jesus and to walk in his footsteps." Its declared object was to shun wealth, ease and luxury, as well as worldly rank and power, the disciples and members to give all the energies of their being to the work they had undertaken. They would be clothed in humble garb, gladly enduring hardships and the reproaches of men, that they might the more effectually labor among the lowly, the degraded, the downtrodden, the ignorant, and the inferior in all lands. And when an order was formed, Francis pledged it to perpetual poverty, that they might not be diverted from their holy mission by earthly pleasures. They avowed a determination to labor for the cause of the divine Master alone, without self-aggrandizement or hope of earthly reward, and to bring to all the degraded and unfortunate the joys of redemption. In 1209 the group numbered twelve. Francis took them to Rome to seek the approval of Pope Innocent III for further development of the order.

Innocent III was a man of many worldly cares. The temporal power of the Church was then tantamount to the power of the rulers of the Western World. Francis of Assisi stood before this great and powerful man, a dusty, barefoot pilgrim in worn garments, and Innocent III lost no time in terminating the interview. But that night the Pope could not sleep. What was it about this simple man's cheerful face that disturbed him? When finally he did slumber he had a dream. In it he viewed the vast structure of the Church shaking violently and about to topple into ruin, until somehow it was firmed and supported from below. Upon close scrutiny he saw that it was Francis who steadied and held up the Church. Next day the Pope recalled Francis and granted him permission to found the Order of the Friars Minor. Francis's followers quickly became known as Little Brothers.

With the blessing of the Pope they went their way rejoicing. They traveled on foot, accepting what was given them as Jesus had done, preaching and comforting the poor and unfortunate. They became learned, knowing that knowledge is power, that they might call it into requisition for the better execution of their task. They studied those practical sciences and arts which would help to meet every emergency that might arise within the scope of their mission. They were temperate in all things, that they might be able to rely on their mental and physical powers in times of trial and danger. They subjected themselves to severe tests and trained all their faculties for success.

Probably no one in history has ever set himself so seriously as did Francis to imitate the life of Christ and to carry out so literally Christ's work in Christ's own way. This is the key to the character and spirit of Saint Francis. Only by accepting completely this truth of Francis can one envision the full portrait of Saint Francis as a lover of nature, a social worker, an itinerant preacher, a lover of poverty. Certainly the love of poverty is part of his spirit; his contemporaries celebrated the "holy nuptials of Francis with Lady Poverty." However, it was not mere external poverty he sought, but the total denial of self.

He considered all nature as a mirror of God and so many steps to God. He called all creatures his "brothers" and "sisters." He even referred to dying as "sister Death." When he visited the village of Gubbio he tamed a savage wolf which had been terrorizing the inhabitants. He addressed the beast very courteously as "Brother Wolf" and exhorted him to leave the villagers in peace, as they bore the wolf no grudge and promised to feed him regularly. Soon the wolf became the town pet. He called the sheep and the fishes his brothers; the doves and the moon and the water his sisters. To little lambs and wild rabbits he gave his special protection. His long and painful illnesses, in later years, were nicknamed his sisters, and he begged pardon of "brother Ass the body."

He once preached a sermon to the birds in a grove beside the road where he had paused to pray. "My little sisters, in your songs you should take care to magnify the Lord, for you are much be-holden to Him for everything. Consider the element of air he has ordained for you, and your wondrous wings that carry you across the world. You neither sow nor reap; but He provides you grain and rain for your drink. You neither spin nor weave; yet He clothes you and your children with feathers. Thank God, therefore, for wings and the breeze, for fountains and fruit, and ever strive to praise Him so that men may hear." Whereupon the birds bowed their heads in reverence until Francis made the sign of the Cross over them and gave them leave to go. They rose up as one flock; and soaring high, they divided into four parts to make a cross in the sky. There they hovered in cross formation, caroling as never before. Then one part of the flock flew east, and others flew west, north and south. And the people who had witnessed the sight un-derstood that Francis and the Little Brothers were like the birds —free, possessing nothing, and wholly dependent upon God's provi-dence, as they scattered in all directions preaching His love.

The Franciscans did not preach in vain. Wherever they went hundreds flocked to hear them, crowds harkened to the inspired words of Francis and his disciples, responded to the pristine sim-plicity and charity of their way of life. Amove all, Francis's deep sense of brotherhood under God embraced his fellow men, for he considered himself no friend of Christ if he did not cherish those for whom Christ died.

As the friars became more numerous, the order extended out-side Italy. In the late spring of 1219 Francis set out for the Holy Land, to "speak with the Moslems and to try to convert them. Although our enemies, they, too, are our brothers whom we love. I shall go to tell them this and beseech them to recognize us as their kin; because we are all of us sons of the Father, and one with humanity. Is it not foolish for brothers to fight and kill one another, even in the name of the cross?"

Francis and two followers sailed for Egypt and made their way to Damietta, which was at that time under siege by the Crusaders. After much trial and many dangers they found the camp of Sala-din, the Moslem warrior prince. Saladin received them with cour-tesy and he heard Francis' plea to end by love the strife between Christian and Moslem. To Saladin this was incomprehensible. When Francis saw that he could not prevail upon Saladin, he of-fered to throw himself into the fire in token of his faith and challenged the Moslem prince to do the same. The offer was rejected, but out of profound respect Saladin gave orders that Francis remain unharmed while in his domain.

Despite Francis's eloquence and genuine affection for these dark brethren, he failed completely to bridge the abyss between the two religions. Giving up, he departed with his two companions and returned to Italy. Thus ended the first foreign mission of the Franciscans—in failure.

Francis became infected by malaria on his journey, and as a result his health began to fail. Moreover a disease he contracted in Egypt dimmed his eyesight and threatened to blot out the world whose beauty he loved as expressions of God's mind. In the summer of 1224 he went to the mountain retreat of La Verna to celebrate the feast of the Assumption of Our Lady. There he prayed that he might best know how to please God. Opening the Gospels for the answer, three times he came upon the references to the Passions of Christ. As he prayed, suddenly he beheld a vision. A figure was coming toward him from the heights of heaven. As the figure stood above him, he saw that it was a man and yet a seraph with six wings; his arms were extended and his feet conjoined, and his body was fixed with a cross. Two wings were raised above his head, two were extended as if in flight, and two covered his whole body. The face was beautiful beyond all earthly beauty, and it smiled gently upon Francis. Conflicting emotions filled his heart, for though the vision brought great joy, the sight of the suffering and crucified figure stirred him to deepest sorrow. Francis pondered long what the vision might mean, then he finally understood. It was God's providence that he would be made like Christ not by a bloody martyrdom but by conformity in mind and heart. When he understood this fully, the vision disappeared, leaving a hot and devoted love in the inner man. Francis looked at himself and saw that the figure had no less marvelously marked him outwardly with the stigmata of the Crucified.

Francis took great care to hide these wounds in his hands and feet during the remainder of his life. He lived but two years longer. In desperate effort to stave off blindness he submitted to unimaginable torture. A red-hot iron was drawn across his eyes to cure the disease that was in them. His pain-racked body was bled many times. These savage treatments were undertaken in the autumn of 1225, when he was forty-three years old.

He lingered until the springtime, when his "brothers" and "sisters," the birds and the blossom-scented flowers, returned to his beloved hills of Portiuncula. He had himself returned there from Sienna, where he had gone for a final treatment. It was an afternoon warm with May when he knew the end was approaching. He begged two of his disciples to lay him bare upon Mother Earth, so that nothing would impede his reunion with her.

From under their brown hoods several of the Little Brothers watched from afar the passing of that tragic and exultant spirit, intoning the words from his *Cantile of the Sun:* "Hail, Sister Death, that openest for me the Gates of Life."

Four centuries later, the followers of this saint, the Franciscan Friars, came to Texas and, with the spirit of Francis of Assisi, established the missions on its soil.

Healing the Indians.

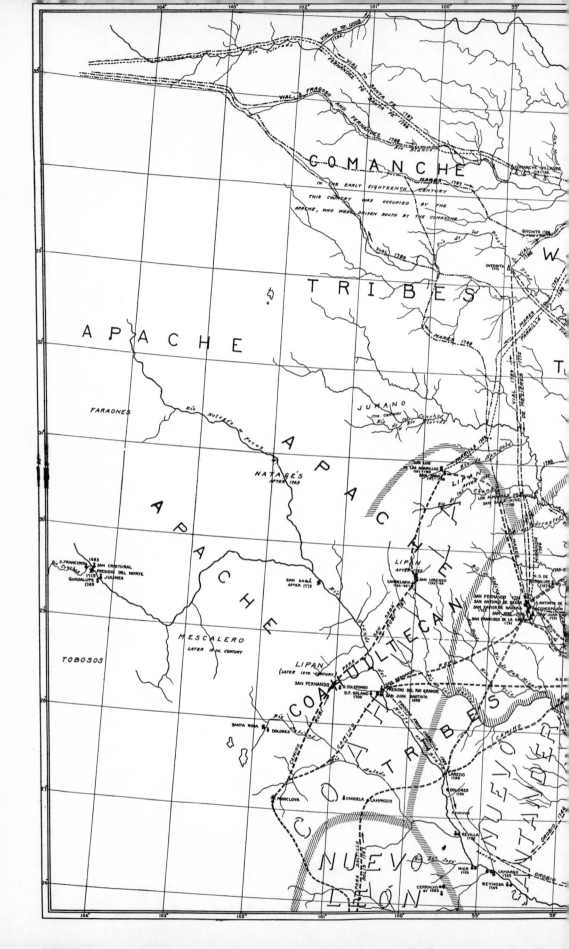

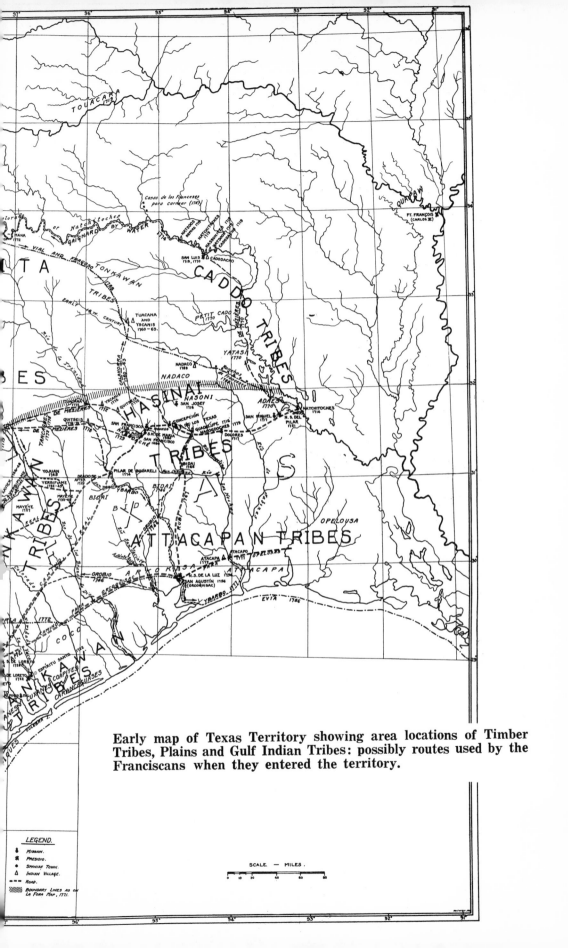

Early map of Texas Territory showing area locations of Timber Tribes, Plains and Gulf Indian Tribes: possibly routes used by the Franciscans when they entered the territory.

LEGEND.

- ⚓ MISSION.
- ✳ PRESIDIO.
- ● SPANISH TOWN.
- △ INDIAN VILLAGE.
- – – – ROAD.
- //////// BOUNDARY LINES AS ON LA FORA MAP, 1771.

SCALE — MILES.

3
Early Inhabitants of Texas

ANTHROPOLOGISTS have recognized for the past century or
longer that, based upon differences in noticeable features of
the body, there are four or five grand divisions of the human race.
The peoples comprising these divisions have different physical,
mental, and moral characteristics which persist in all climes and
under all conditions. They differ so widely as to be classified into
separate races. As a result the world has become familiar with the
crude classification of humanity into the following groups: Cau-
casian, Negro, Malay, Mongolian, and the American Indian.

The American Indian, first classified as the fifth grand division
or race of man, is now considered in scientific classification as a
subdivision of the Mongolian race. The Mongolian tribes of Asia
were very numerous and widely dispersed. In later times they were
known to wander, in many tribes, over adjacent islands of the New
World. While conclusive evidence is still lacking, it is accepted that
the North American Indian is a descendant of one or more of
these ancient tribes. No conjecture has yet been made as to the
time when their ancestral tribes parted company. However, recent
intensive research into Mongol and American Indian language,
habit, mentality, dress, mode of life and livelihood, religious atti-
tudes, and so forth have led the anthropologist to the reasonable
assumption that they have a common or related origin.

A tribe discovered in Hindustan, and traced back to the ancient
Mongols, has such strong physical resemblance to the American
Indian as to be certainly recognized as a congenital race. Their
implements seem to be made on the same model: fire sticks, tobacco
pipes, and primitive pottery—with zigzag ornamental lines. So, also,
is their style of dress somewhat similar, the same disposition of
beads and ornament. Morever, their mode of housing—the use of

huts and tents were on one easily recognized model. The democratic system of their tribal governments, their social equality and communal rights of property, all were alike. Their ideas of disease and remedies, their charms and incantations were either learned in the same nescient school or sprang from some innate cast of thought and disposition. The list of minute identities of customs and actions might be greatly extended. Many of them, no doubt, sprang from like circumstances producing the same effects. Somewhat similar customs are observed in all savage races, but minute identities, when greatly multiplied, as were found to be among the American Indian tribes and the Mongol tribes, can only be explained by a theory of common origin.

The Mongol rule of warfare, being an indiscriminate massacre of all ages, sexes and conditions, was everywhere the same; however, with the Indian tribes, this was somewhat modified as time progressed. It became the Indians' universal custom to make prisoners of small children, who were adopted into the tribe as equal members of it. Once adopted, there was no race prejudice, and no caste to hinder perfect equality. This custom of carrying children into captivity and adopting them into the tribe was followed in their warfare with the white people; and notwithstanding the specific differences of race and the violent contrast in the mode of life of the whites and the Indians, there was in the wild life of the savage a charm so potent that after a few years the captive did not wish to return to civilization. Women, also, were more often captured than slain. Nor were men by any means always massacred. Sometimes they were spared, to be dismissed with contemptuous indifference, sometimes from the better motives of admiration for their courage, sometimes from friendly motives. It is easy to think for the Indian, but to think with him requires a different cast of mind from the white man's, or a skill not yet attained. The wild tribes of Texas, it has been asserted, never spared from motives of compassion or pity; but this charge will not apply to all the Texas tribes, as we shall see.

It has been customary to think of the American Indian as nomadic, without fixed homes, wandering at will over the face of the country. This is a mistake. Whenever they did wander, it was always temporary—and unusual. The Indians, as a rule, had fixed homes and a permanent territory within which each tribe dwelt. The district was often extensive and indefinite in its boundaries;

within its limits the Indians were accustomed to wander widely and frequently, thus the first settlers assumed the Indians to be nomadic peoples. With the introduction of horses by the Spaniards, the means and the inducements for traveling great distances were multiplied, and the tribal movements became correspondingly more frequent and extensive. The knowledge and use of firearms likewise rendered the Indians more restless and mobile, by offering them temptations to war and the chase. These two influences, the horse and the gun, were very powerful among most of the tribes.

The Indians of Texas were not numerous. In proportion to the territory occupied by them, they were scattered and few. Had all the Indians living in Texas territory when the Spaniards came been brought together, they probably would not have formed a city one fourth the size of Waco, which has a population of about 100,000.

These Indians, for the sake of simplicity and as far as dealing with them in relation to the missions, can be grouped into three general divisions: the Timber tribes, the Plains tribes, and the Coast tribes. All told, historians have listed a total of 162 Indian tribes that inhabited Texas at the time of the coming of the Franciscan fathers. The habitat of these tribes formed a half moon extending from the southern portion of Texas, following its eastern frontier and extending along its northern extremities. Language has come to be recognized as the only sure basis for a correct scientific test of race kinship, and upon real identities of speech is founded the arrangement into tribes, groups and families.

The most advanced of the Texas Indians were the Timber Indians. Linguistically these may be divided into two main divisions— the Hasinai and the Caddo proper. The Hasinai lived on the Angelina and the upper Neches rivers, and comprised some ten or more tribes. They lived in large conical grass lodges, in scattered agricultural villages, and raised good crops of maize, beans, pumpkins, and sunflowers. They varied their diet with fish, small game, bear and deer.

Tejas was a common word of greeting, meaning "friend," by which members of this group of Indians addressed each other. Unaware of this fact, the Spaniards applied this name to all the tribes of eastern Texas when they first came in contact with them in the early 1680's. But the industrious and painstaking Father Francisco de Jesue Maria Casañas, a close and intelligent observer, soon discovered the mistake and pointed out that the Indians of the region did not constitute a "Great Kingdom of Texas" as was thought, and that the real name of the group was not Tejas (Texas). The idea persisted, however, and in time came to designate the entire province with its changing boundaries and ever increasing area. The language of these Indians, though, has definitely established them as being a branch of the Caddoan stock.

The Hasinai Indians are described as having been sedentary and amenable to the friars' instructions. Captain Juan Dominguez Mendoza's description of them contains the following: "The main attribute of the male is, as a rule, fierce bravery, while the women possess a softness and femininity, pathetic when seen in the light of their insecure lives. They are beautiful, white and graceful and very affable without being lacking in honesty: and especially they are modest with strangers. At all seasons of the year they dress with much decorum. . . . They are so fore-sighted that at whatever hour of the day a guest might arrive, they immediately present him with a platter of food. . . . Finally, they are affable, docile and pious and if they could be gotten away from the old men who are filled with superstition to the marrow of their bones, their conversion to Christianity would not be difficult." It might be noted, also, that had it not been for the continual harassment of the French over the disputed frontier in eastern Texas, the labors of the friars with these Indians might have borne greater fruit.

West of the Timber tribes, on the great prairies and plains, over a great area roamed wandering tribes who nevertheless regarded some particular part of the country as their own. These were the Plains tribes. They were tall, straight, well-formed, robust, of lordly bearing, with regular features, and possessing a high order of intelligence. The Plains Indians were numerous, but the most important of these were the Apache (meaning "enemy"), which roughly were divided into the Lipan and Mescalero tribes. They are described as being fierce and warlike, astute and bold, but false and perfidious, and enemies of all things. "One may rest assured that in their vile hearts they prefer a horse or mule to even their own parents, children, and women. They are clean and decent in dress, but of lascivious customs. Ruthless and heartless, the Apache is hated alike by all tribes. His hand is against every man and every man's hand is against him." This is how Colonel Diego Ortiz Parilla, co-founder of San Saba Mission, sized up the Apache-Lipan tribe of Indians.

To these Indians the buffalo was all-important. Besides furnishing the staple food, it provided a variety of other important commodities. The brains and liver were used for softening leather, the horns and skull for ladles and vessels, the shoulder blades for hoes or picks, the tendons for bow strings, the tail hair to make ropes and belts, the hide to provide bridle and saddle and to furnish shields, tents, traveling cases, shirts, moccasins, beds, and robes—a surprising array of gifts from one clumsy beast.

The Apaches ranged from the Pecos to the Rio Grande, their real home being in the mountains of Mexico, New Mexico, and Arizona. The Comanches, hereditary foes of the Apaches, often sought to outdo their rivals in cruelty and savagery. The Apaches and Comanches at times professed a disposition for peace and civilization, but invariably relapsed into savagery, sometimes forming a temporary alliance to attack the missions and pueblos. Their history is a bloody and ferocious record in Texas, as well as in Mexico and other places.

It was for the Apache Indians that the San Saba Mission was founded. The attempt to befriend this cruel and fierce nation was a mistake, which, had it been avoided, would likely have assured success for the northern missions. When the Apaches, assisted by a band of Comanches, massacred the padres in San Saba mission, it signaled the end of the Franciscans' attempt to civilize and Christianize the North Texas Indians.

The Coast tribes' habitat was the Gulf Coast, from Saint Joseph Island near Aransas Pass to the vicinity of Galveston Bay. The men are described by Carlos Castenada in *Our Catholic Heritage in Texas* as "tall and well-formed; their women shorter and fleshier; their hair was very coarse, and the men usually wore it long, reaching sometimes as low as their waist. They were frequently at war with the interior tribes, and were, from their first contact with Europeans to the end of the Spanish regime, regarded as particularly dangerous to mariners of that perilous coast, with not a few of them succumbing to the Indians' savage attacks. Their appetite for human flesh is attested to by all who came in contact with them from the time of Cabeza de Vaca to as late as the Anglo-American period of colonization."

The largest group of Coast tribes with whom the Franciscan fathers had to deal were the Karankawans, who lived in the region extending from the area that today comprises Chambers County to the present Nueces County. Other tribes of the Karankawans were the Coco, the Ceyone, the Coapite, the Copane, and the Carancaguases. An early friar's account, as quoted by Castenada, of the Carancaguases described them thus: "This tribe is unique in gluttony. They eagerly eat locusts, lice, and even human flesh. Their appetite does not require seasoning. They eat raw meat, tallow, bear's fat; and with all this they show a great passion for spoiled food; they eat their dried fish crawling with worms. These Indians are very dirty and the stench which they emit is enough to turn one's stomach. They are fond of all that is pestiferous and for this reason delight in the odor of the polecat and eat its flesh, often without cooking it. . . . Some of these Indians practice the basest types of immorality with each other. . . . They exceed all others in cruelty to captives; they also surpass all others in cowardliness and vileness. They unpardonably takes the lives of the old of both sexes whom they capture, eat the children, sell the boys, and sacrifice the soldiers and the strong to their false gods. They lash the victims to a stake, then build a huge fire around them. They dance around the fire, all carrying a sharpened knife of iron or flint or pieces of shell. When they see fit they approach a captive, slice off a piece of flesh, pass it over the fire as part of the ritual, and, dripping with blood, they eat it in sight of the victim, accompanying this with horrible gestures and inhuman voices. They continue this macabre ritual until the victim dies and is eaten, then they divide the bones among themselves. Sometimes they forsake the ritual and hang the captive by his feet and roast him over a fire and slowly eat him. Whenever they capture an enemy who has taken lives of their braves, they do not trouble to use knives, but tear off flesh with their teeth and eat it bit by bit, until the victim dies before their blood-drenched faces."

These, then, were the Texas Indians, whose history is blended with the missionary work of the Franciscans. They were a different breed from the much advanced Aztecs and Incas with whom the Spaniards had dealt in Mexico. They were a strange and primitive and ofttimes hostile people who were utterly ignorant, not only of the moral code of elevated society but also of the rights of property. As Christianity and civilization must necessarily flourish together, the Indians had to be civilized as well as converted. They had to be taught to love God more than their hunting ground, and to forgive their enemies and not to eat them. They had to be taught

a new language, to become domesticated, to understand the nature
of property, its value, and the proper mode of acquiring it. But
what was more important, it was necessary for the Indian to un-
learn all he had previously acquired. His passions must be subdued; his habits, manners, and his entire nature changed. These
teachings were to be the result of infinite patience, constant prayer,
and a living faith. It was an exceedingly difficult task to undertake;
indeed, it was a seemingly impossible task.

Who then was sufficient for these things? The Jesuits, cheerful,
polished and courtly, chose California with its golden sunshine,
skies of ineffable blue, and with its gardens of olive, myrtle, the
orange, and the vine; the Dominicans, as preachers against heretics,
were gloomy and fanatical, and eschewed the rigors of Texas and
the fierceness of the Karankawans, Apaches, and Comanches. But
the patient followers of Saint Francis of Assisi—they came, and
here they found they could well keep their vows of virtue and self-
denial. Here they found what they eternally sought—souls to save.

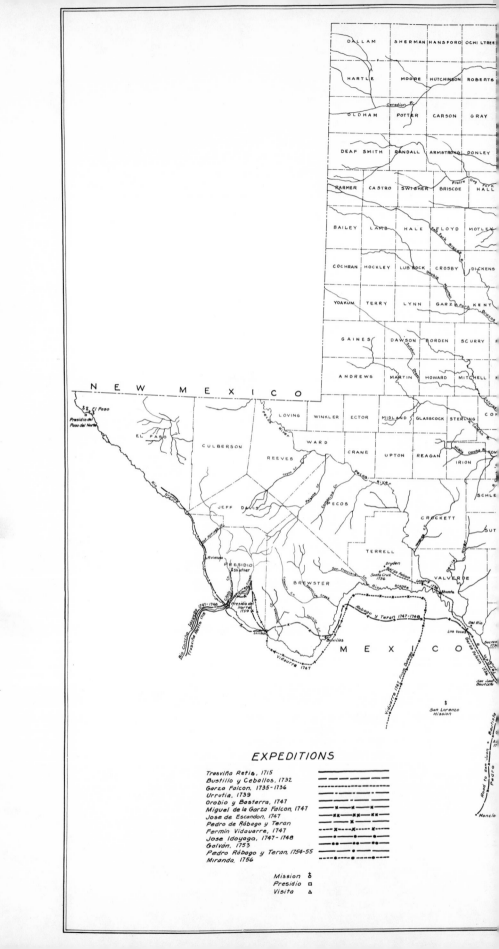

EXPEDITIONS

Trasviña Retis, 1715	
Bustillo y Ceballos, 1732	
Garza Falcon, 1735-1736	
Urrutia, 1739	
Orobio y Basterra, 1747	
Miguel de la Garza Falcon, 1747	
Jose de Escandon, 1747	
Pedro de Rábago y Teran	
Fermín Vidauarre, 1747	
Jose Idoyaga, 1747-1748	
Galván, 1753	
Pedro Rábago y Teran, 1754-55	
Miranda, 1756	

Mission ŏ
Presidio □
Visita △

ap of Texas Territory showing locations of some of the early
issions and presidios.

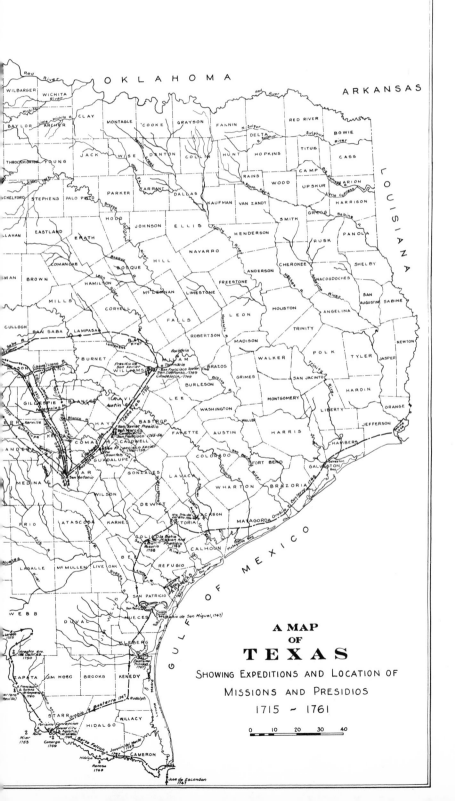

A MAP
OF
TEXAS
SHOWING EXPEDITIONS AND LOCATION OF
MISSIONS AND PRESIDIOS
1715 - 1761

0   10   20   30   40

4

Old Texas as a Mission Field

THE name Texas is derived from the Indian words *Ticlas* and *Theas*, through the Spanish form *Tejas*. Its meaning has been translated variously as "friend," "ally," "paradise," and "land of tents." The early American colonizers corrupted the Spanish name Tejas as Texias, calling themselves Texians, and later to Texas and Texans. Tejas became the name given to a large Indian federation inhabiting the vast region extending as far as Wyoming and encompassing parts of what is today New Mexico, Kansas, and Colorado. The region of present-day Texas, though greatly diminished from the original, comprises a twelfth of the area of conterminous United States.

Geologically it tilts to the southeast, as if propped up against the western mountains. Thus its streams flow from northwest to southeast, almost parallel with each other. Eight of them—the Sabine, Neches, Trinity, Brazos, Colorado, Guadalupe–San Antonio, Nueces, and Rio Grande—empty into the Gulf of Mexico. The Rio Grande, longest of the rivers, forms the southwestern boundary of Texas. The Red River, second longest and the only one of importance not bearing a Spanish name, is part of the northern boundary, and the Sabine is part of the eastern boundary. Because of its fortuitous location and because of its enormous area, a fact so obvious as to be neglected when Texas is compared to any other state, the area is subjected to a diversity of extreme climates, the northern portion reaching into a frigid zone and the southern portion extending into the tropical zone.

Man has been traced through fifteen thousand years of the area's history. However, historically—the time in which people of European origin have known the land that became Texas—the state's history began in the sixteenth century. European man did not find existence easy in Texas country: he suffered the bitter cold and the intolerable heat, he countenanced floods and droughts, tornadoes and hurricanes; he was scourged by the praying mantis, scorpion, black tarantula, and red ants; he fell victim to man-eating animals and died of the poison of rattlesnakes, coral snakes, copperheads, and water moccasins. Could civilized man and his niceties replace the things repulsive that thrived on this hard bosom of primitive land?

Wherever there is land or water or air, and the promise of reward of riches, man has penetrated and existed. More recently he has ventured where there is no land or water or air—and managed to exist. Therefore one should not marvel at European man's conquest of Texas, though one might wonder at the shifting allegiance of Texans. Visitors who are asked about the six flags the state has flown over the land will name them in this order: Spanish, French, Mexican, Texan (Lone Star, for the Republic of Texas), American, Confederate. A careful examination of the history of the exploration and settlement of Texas territory discloses that this order of appearance may not be technically correct, because of the dispute over the arrangement existing between Spain and France.

Spain declared herself the lawful owner of Texas for three reasons: the discovery of America by Columbus; the conquest of Mexico, of which Texas was considered a part; and the explorations of various Spanish discoverers. The explorers were Álvar Núñez Cabeza de Vaca who, with three companions, sole survivors of a wrecked ship, were washed up on the Gulf coast in 1528; Hernando de Soto, searching for mythical cities of gold and gems, whose expedition passed the spot where Texarkana now stands, probably in 1543; and Francisco Vasquez de Coronado, who departed Mexico about the same time, also seeking the fabled country of Cibola—of the Seven Cities whose streets were said to be literally paved with pure gold blocks—lying off to the north. (Hadn't Cortez found fabulously rich cities farther to the south, in Mexico?) There are legends affirming that Coronado's expedition was successful and, fearing the hostile Gulf Indian tribes, that he buried treasures of gold, silver, and gems somewhere east of the Rio Grande. From time to time stories come to light of portions of Coronado's treasure trove being unearthed. The search goes on continually without publicity. Ranchers have been known to lease "mineral" rights on their land to these diggers, retaining a portion of the find for themselves.

The French claim to Texas lay principally with the enterprises of René Robert Cavalier, Sieur de La Salle: his discoveries in the Mississippi River territory and his settlement and explorations in Texas. After six years of persistent effort he had succeeded in navigating the Mississippi River to its mouth. On April 9, 1682, he formally claimed the Mississippi River with all the territory drained by its tributaries for the king of France. In his declaration he laid claim to a monstrous portion of North America . . . "from the mouth of the great river, on the eastern side, otherwise called Ohio . . . as far as its mouth at the sea, or Gulf of Mexico, about the twenty-seventh degree of elevation of the North Pole, *and also to the mouth of the River of Palms.*" (Italics are the author's.) By his last phrase he laid claim to the vast empire of Texas and so laid the foundation of endless diplomatic wrangles over the limits of Louisiana.

Two years later La Salle received a commission from the king of France to establish a colony at the mouth of the Mississippi. On July 24, 1684, his little fleet of four vessels sailed from La Rochelle, France, with a group of four hundred persons. He missed the mouth of the Mississippi, perhaps deliberately, and sailed on around the coast of Texas, and landed on the west side of Matagorda Bay. After scouting the country, he selected a site about six miles up the Garcitas Creek and established Fort Saint Louis. La Salle's journal says: "Between the palisades and the stream lay a narrow strip of marsh, the haunt of countless birds; and at a distance it deepened into pools full of fish. All the surrounding prairies swarmed with game. . . . The river supplied our colonists with turtles and the bay with oysters."

For the next two years La Salle explored the territory, making expeditions into the eastern wilderness and onto the western plains. On March 20, 1687, he was shot and killed by one of his own men, somewhere in the vicinity of the present city of Columbus, Texas.

By all the rules, then, of natural law, the country was French and, if they chose to call it so, a part of Louisiana. The country was French by right of discovery. The Spanish voyagers Ponce de Leon, Narvaez, De Ayllón, and De Soto had never seen any part of the vast extent of seacoast between Cape Florida and Soto de la Marina. The pretensions and claims set up by Spain to this country, because she was in possession of these extreme points, are not supported by any of the rules of national law established by the governments of Europe in regard to their American discoveries.

The rules were: (1) that when any European nation takes possession of any extent of seacoast, that possession is understood as extending into the interior country to the source of the rivers emptying within that coast, to the exclusion of all other nations to the same; (2) that whenever one European nation makes a discovery, and takes possession of any portion of this continent, and another afterwards does the same at some distance from it, where the boundary between them is not determined by the principle above mentioned, that the middle distance becomes such, of course; (3) that whenever any European nation has thus acquired a right to any portion of territory on this continent, that right can never be diminished or affected by any other power, by virtue of purchases made, by grants, or conquests of the natives, within the limits thereof.

The French colony of La Salle, tested by these indisputable rules of natural equity, were thus upon French soil, which was Texas territory.

Phillip II of Spain, realizing the shakiness of his claim to the Texas territory, issued a royal order forbidding, on pain of death, any foreigner to sail on the Gulf. At the same time he found it necessary to reaffirm Spain's claim to Texas territory by calling attention to a Papal Bull, issued by Pope Alexander VI in 1499, which purported to settle the dispute between Portugal and Spain concerning their claims in America by dividing their conquests by a line running from pole to pole 370 miles west of the Azores, which confirmed to Spain the territory west of that meridian.

Here, then, in the discoveries of La Salle and by his settlement in Texas, under orders from his sovereign, and the pretensions of Spain, was laid the foundation of a controversy which was settled only in 1762 when France ceded Louisiana west of the Mississippi to Spain. (In 1800 it was ceded back to France.) Therefore, for a full century, from the year 1680 until 1762, Texas was in truth under *two* flags—French and Spanish.

After August 24, 1821, when Juan O'Donoju, the representative of the Spanish king, signed the treaty of Cordoba, which recognized the independence of Mexico, Texas came under the Mexican banner. After the battle at San Jacinto in 1836, Texas, flying its famous "Lone Star" flag, became a republic. In 1845 it joined the United States and flew the Stars and Stripes. On January 28, 1861, by a vote in the state assembly of 166 "ayes" to seven "nays"—including General Sam Houston's—Texas withdrew from the Union and fought under the Confederate flag. Although the Civil War officially ended April 9, 1865, the war did not come to a close until five weeks later when the last shot was fired on Texas soil May 13 at Palmeto on the Rio Grande.

Some Texans are wont to claim a seventh flag. The red-petticoat flag of Mrs. James Long, sometimes called "The Mother of Texas," was raised at Point Bolivar in 1821. Between the purchase of Louisiana in 1803 and the agreement on the boundary question in 1819, more than one band of adventurers made their way into Texas. Dr. James Long of Natchez, Mississippi, marched with a force of volunteers into Texas and occupied Nacogdoches. At a meeting there, Long was elected president of the new republic. He then set out for Galveston to try to induce the pirate Jean Laffite to join his forces and help put the Spanish forces out of Texas territory. Laffite refused, and during Dr. Long's absence a strong Spanish force fell upon the poorly led and ill-equipped Americans at Nacogdoches and routed them.

Dr. Long had seen the vision of an American Texas and he was not easily turned aside. In 1821 he returned to Texas by way of the mouth of the San Antonio River, with an army of about sixty men. He left his wife, Jane, her small daughter Ann, and a few soldiers at Point Bolivar across the channel from Galveston Island, while he and his army attacked the bastion of La Bahia at Goliad on the San Antonio River. The fort was captured, but after a few days the invaders were forced to surrender and taken to San Antonio. Dr. Long was transferred to a prison in Mexico City, but was given his freedom after Mexican independence was assured. Soon after his release from prison, however, and while in Mexico City, he was killed by a Mexican soldier.

Meanwhile, Mrs. Jane Long bravely held out at Point Bolivar although Long's soldiers had deserted, and a second daughter was born to her during the winter. Fortunately for the little group the Indians did not know that Mrs. Long, her two daughters, and a twelve-year-old Negro servant girl were alone. Mrs. Long was careful to keep a flag—her red flannel petticoat—flying, and each morning she fired a small cannon that had been left at the fort. She was finally rescued by settlers on their way to Austin's colony.

Jane Long lived many years and devoted her life to the cause of Texas independence.

When Hernando Cortez in 1519 set out from Cuba to seize the hoarded wealth of the civilized Aztecs, he carried with him to the new continent the Franciscan friars. This was in accordance with a provision of Pope Alexander VI's Bull which specified that the natives of the Western world would be instructed in the Catholic faith. By 1522 Cortez had seized the Aztec gold and treasure, and henceforth Mexico served as the base for Spanish expeditions that explored and colonized the lands to the north. The Spanish adventurers hoped to find hoards of gold, silver, and other treasure in these lands. The Franciscan padres who accompanied them sought only souls to Christianize and minds to civilize; for to these intrepid people the human soul was the most precious possession in life. The Spaniards found only brown and mostly barren lands and, in most instances, hostile Indians. The Franciscans found what they came seeking.

The means employed by the Spanish to colonize the Western world was twofold: religious and political. Indeed, throughout the two thousand years of Western history political rulers have used the machinery of the Church to carry out their work, whether benevolent or destructive. Notwithstanding, the friars joined hands with the Spaniards in all their conquests. In no case was success achieved save where the commercial and social relations of the natives blended with the religious and political. The politicians dominated the scene in Texas, yet the padres went about their task with equanimity, regardless of the sometimes abusive dominance of the conquistadores, and they were most successful. After a hundred and forty years the Spanish withdrew never to return: they left little more than their language and the mark of the conquistadores' sword. But the Franciscan friars planted the cross in Texas and their labors have propagated and bear an ever increasing abundance of the fruit of their wonderful heritage. Tribe after tribe of Indians abandoned their gods and followed the way of the friars. And the Franciscan way of life spread to other peoples of the New World. Missions built by the barefoot, brown-robed Little Brothers, intent on saving souls, still stand as monuments to their patience, their culture, and to their zeal.

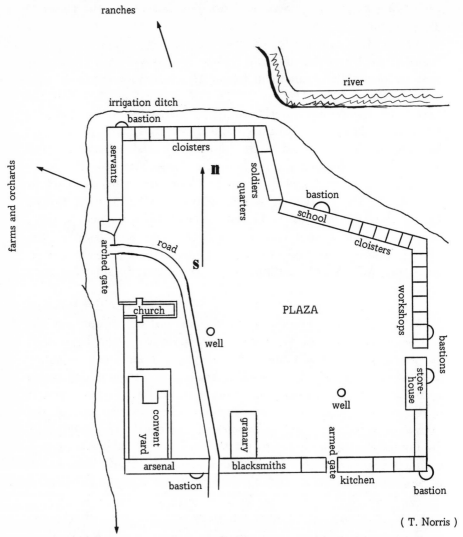

ranches

river

irrigation ditch

bastion

cloisters

servants

soldiers quarters

bastion

school

cloisters

n

farms and orchards

s

road

workshops

arched gate

bastions

church

PLAZA

well

store-house

convent yard

well

granary

arsenal   blacksmiths   armed gate   kitchen

bastion   bastion

(T. Norris)

Ground plan of an old Texas mission, showing the relatively small
portion of the works the chapel or church constituted. The chapel
was usually the last structure raised. The storehouse, the granary,
the workshops and school quarters were considered more important
for the beginning of a mission. Today the chapel or church portion
is usually in the best condition of all other sections of an old mission.

5
The Mission and Its Function

TO comprehend fully the character and function of the old mission, it is necessary to also understand the presidio and the pueblo in relation to the mission. The strength of the entire Spanish colonial scheme rested on the foundation of outposts on a pattern which involved the parallel growth of presidio, pueblo, and the mission. The early Texas mission, more properly defined, can be described as "mission system," consisting of three main elements, each necessary to the other for existence. There was the mission itself, which was a combined church, school, and factory of a sort; there was the pueblo, which was the village where the Indians lived; and there was the presidio, the garrison for the officers and soldiers who protected the mission system.

Much of the literature of the old missions of Texas is highly idealized, and the mission institution has been made to appear romantic rather than as the governmental agency it was, which combined the religious and the cultural and the practical. The missions were supported by the royal treasury to serve the state's purpose, and as viewed by the government the work of the missionaries was to assist in extending, holding, Christianizing, and civilizing the frontiers. But the Sons of Saint Francis put their apostolic zeal before all else, although they were most useful explorers and diplomatic agents. The mission, a frontier institution, was not designed to be permanent. In theory it was temporary and transistory. Also in theory the missionaries were allowed a period of ten years to Christianize and civilize the natives; and then they were supposed to move father on or go to a new frontier where they could start their work all over again. However this plan was only haphazardly adhered to in Texas.

The mission itself was primarily a church or friary, but it was

43

much more; it was also a school of industry, agriculture, and government. The mission commonly was constructed on a quadrangle design, embracing a group of small houses or rooms, sometimes called cloisters, which housed padres and lay brothers, their neatly whitewashed cells opening onto arcades bordering the garden patio. Built off on another side would be the rooms to house the soldiers assigned to the mission for its protection and the servants for the assistance of the missionaries. Another group of buildings located in the area would house the Indian neophytes and provide space for the kilns, the granary, the looms, the tailor shop, the carpenter shop, and the blacksmith shop. These various units were generally enclosed within a protecting wall, with fortified gates and entrances. Beyond the enclosed pueblo or Indian village, for that is precisely what a mission was, were the fields cultivated by the Indians. These were normally irrigated by ditches, dug by the Indians. Beyond the cultivated fields the mission had its ranch, where the stock, the sheep and the goats, the asses and mules, and the oxen were cared for on suitable grazing lands. So, as we can see, the church formed a nucleus for the walled-in Indian community, called a pueblo.

The presidio was nothing less than the barracks compound or fort within or near a settlement where the garrison and its officers were quartered. The secular administrators also resided there. As a protection and to impress the Indians with a sense of respect, it was customary to establish a presidio a short distance from the mission, or a group of missions, as was done in eastern Texas and in the area of what is today San Antonio. The garrisons stationed in the presidios not only afforded protection to the mission against hostile Indians, but they served to hold the frontier in case of aggression. The garrisons furnished a small number of soldiers to each mission to help the padres instruct the neophytes.

These soldiers were a source of continual annoyance to the friars. Usually of a low and often criminal class, the soldiers took it as their license to ravish the Indian maidens at will. The missionaries repeatedly demanded married soldiers but rarely, if ever, got them. The fathers drew up charges against the soldiers who, aside from molesting the young female neophytes by their licentious conduct, outraged the natives and drove them to hate the white man. The soldiers, in defiance, drew up countercharges against the friars. At every turn the missionaries were baffled by the soldiers and opposed by the officers and politicians who supported the military. However, the Franciscans never for a moment forgot that their principal purpose, often overlooked by the military, was to befriend and convert the Indians.

The Indians, accustomed to being the masters of their own time, found life in the missions tedious, and it required much persuasion and ingenuity on the part of the missionaries to keep them from running away, as indeed they often did. At dawn they were required to attend religious services, after which they gathered in front of the church for a period of religious instruction in the catechism. Although the missionaries were required to learn the language of the Indians among whom they worked (a requirement not always demanded), religious drills were conducted in the Spanish language. Instruction over, the Indians had their breakfast, after which they were led to the fields either by one of the padres or one of the soldiers assigned to the mission. Often the soldier forced his attention one one or more of the young maidens along the way. Although a majority of the neophytes were taken out to the fields, some went to the workshops, where they learned different trades. While the women made pottery or baskets or worked the looms or busied themselves preparing the meal for those out in the fields, the children went to school. In the evening the entire group gathered in front of the church for another hour of instruction and the rosary.

If the Indians were to become either worthy Christians or desirable subjects they must be disciplined in the rudiments of organized society. Therefore the missionaries were also teachers of social and political science, in a way. They taught the Indians to govern themselves after the pattern of democratic affairs. Thus each pueblo had its Indian governor and councilmen. They also had their sheriffs and deputies, whose principal duty was to see that every Indian congregated for church services in the morning and in the evening. If they failed to attend without a good reason, the culprits were publicly given one to five lashes. Much judgment and discretion was exercised by the unselfish padres, and the Indians learned to manage their own offices, respect property rights, and to worship God.

Under the sympathetic care of the Franciscans a great many Indians learned to manage their own affairs. How successful this phase of missionary life was developed may be judged by a report from the files of San Jose mission, dated 1758. "The kind treatment of the missionaries has so pleased the natives that the best proof of their contentment is that there have been no fugitives, and that there are no chains or stocks in this mission. The neophytes elect their own city council, judges, and councilors, their captain, officers, and governor, and their public prosecutor. At night they have regular guards who make the rounds. They have their military and civil tribunals which administer justice without bloodshed."

The Franciscan fathers sent into Texas were trained for their work at three mission colleges, with seats in Mexico, each one of which sent out occasional inspectors into the northern system. The missions were grouped into "presidencies," which was an offshoot of the earliest development of ritual under the *presidence* of the Church of Rome, and in local affairs each missionary was responsible to his own head. The colleges were Queretaro, Zacatecas, and San Fernando. The missions of the Rio Grande and some on the San Antonio were Queretaran; many of those in eastern Texas and others on the San Antonio were Zacatecan. The San Fernando college was the last to be established and furnished missionaries for a few of the missions ministering to the Apaches and Comanches. Christianizing these Indians proved to be a risky business. As will be seen later, many good Franciscan fathers lost their lives in the effort. Among them Father Alonzo Giraldo de Terreros and Father Jose de Santiesteban, along with others, were ruthlessly murdered by the Indian massacres of Mission San Saba in 1758.

Upon orders from the viceroy, a mission could be secularized whenever it was deemed that the work of the missionaries was completed. Secularization meant that the lands and mission property, except that needed for community purposes and expansion, were to be equally divided among the inhabitants of the mission pueblo. The Indians were to enjoy all the civil rights enjoyed by the Spaniards, but no Indian was allowed to mortgage or endanger the possession of the newly acquired property. They were then taken from under the wing of the Franciscans and entrusted to the secular (layman) authority. By this act of granting civil rights to the Indians they were suddenly deprived of their greatest blessing —the moral and civic support of the fatherly Franciscans.

Throughout the mission era in Texas it may be said that the strongest urge in the exploration and settlement of this territory was wealth and glory. Renown and easy fortune was the ruling passion of the stern conquistadores. As we have seen, the missionary endeavors of the Franciscans in Texas was bound inextricably with the civil settlement and the establishment of military outposts in that inhospitable province. When the conquistadores found no hoards of gold and gems and became dismayed, it was the padres who became heroic men. It was they, inspired by a consuming love that knew no bounds, who could not tear themselves away, could not bring themselves to abandon the wretched, ignorant, idolatrous natives. It was they who persevered against indolence, indifference, perfidy, and ingratitude to maintain the missions and induce Spanish officials to continue their efforts in Texas. They remained, and planted the cross in the wilderness. It may well be doubted that in this later age we have men of such courage.

The Alhambra and Sierra Nevada.

The architecture of Texas missions reflect strongly the Moorish
influence, which motif the Franciscan Fathers brought to the New
World; the Moorish loveliness is especially to be noticed in the
detailed carvings and the portals and windows of the old missions,
as seen here in this view of the famous Alhambra.

6

Architecture of the
Old Missions

T HE sources for the architecture of the Texas missions lie basic-
ally in Spain, which acted as a clearing house for many styles
and motifs, the dominant of which were: Moorish, Romanesque,
Gothic, Renaissance. In describing the characteristic architecture
of the Texas missions it should be remembered that the colonizing
and building was done by people of one nationality, the Spanish;
it was also the expression of one single religious order, the Franciscans.

The contribution of the Moors to the art of mission-building in
Texas is discernible in the field of ornament and decoration. Their
oriental love of lavish detail and brilliant color was unbounded,
sweeping from entire walls of complicated snowflake and geometric
patterns to ceilings where stalactite motifs hung down in a bewil-
dering maze, their crevices and moldings picked out in gold, red,
and blue. They had a great fondness for concentrating on doorway
and window embellishment. They left great stretches of uninter-
rupted plaster walls free of decoration, and let loose a torrent of
form and color at windows and portals.

The French Romanesque influence on the architecture of the
Southwestern missions can be found most readily in the structural
points. Thick massiveness and solid, low-lying forms denote the
Romanesque taste. From this scheme were borrowed the barrel
vaults, square, groined masonry vaults, the buttress, and even the
pierced gable in the openings, such as bell towers. Many other details were the legacy of Spanish Romanesque; most notably the
mark of this era was left on the Texas missions in the simple cruciform shape, which was followed in some variation in almost all of
these structures.

Gothic architecture reached Spain by way of France, and emerged there as a decorative, ornate, and cosmopolitan style. The padres from Spain brought to the New World their memories of gargoyles, flying buttresses, and high pointed vaults, and a love for daring, mysterious interiors and soaring symbolic towers. The Gothic imprint also may be noted in the attempt at massiveness of impression. In Texas this was blended in thickness and strength, made functional in this frontier land.

When the Renaissance reached Spain (1450–1750) it took command of the architecture of other periods and blended both classic and medieval forms into a truly Spanish melange. It wrought a tangle of decorative excitement which satisfied every Latin temperament and left each church priest with a taste for its romance. The mission builders retained the structure borrowed from earlier sources, but moldings and carvings, an entire catalogue of architectural forms from broken pediments to curved and steepled gables, infinitely fine-sculptured detail and round low domes, they lifted from the Renaissance and brought with them to Texas by way of Mexico.

It is fitting that Mexico should have added something to mission building as it extended up into the north. The above forms did not reach Texas in their pure styles. In Mexico they all underwent a new period of gestation and rebirth, and emerged, above the Rio Grande, as really bastard styles but with added native charm. Architectural activity in Mexico was extensive during the period of Spanish occupation. There the forms were overlaid with the lavish employment of the decorative arts. Inspired by the decadence of the Baroque, Mexico added its tumbling form and unrestrained bursts of ornament, blended with natural environmental motifs lending to the Texas mission architecture the lush and almost exotic expression of a southern race. Seen in Texas mission architecture is the imprimatur of Europe's golden age of architectural development, rehatched and reborn in the New World.

In early Texas, contrary to common belief, the church was not always the first structure of the mission to be built. The first consideration of the missionaries was, understandably, security; and so they began with a group of lay buildings which safely enclosed a patio. Mass was necessarily said in a makeshift way until construction of the church or chapel. In addition to providing protection in case of attack, the patio served another and important function. It answered the necessity of the padres' constant supervision over all the buildings and their inmates. Standing in the center of such a courtyard a padre superior could watch the activity of the mission and command attention from any quarter. The padres, being men of refinement and taste, made it one of their first duties to make the patio beautiful as well. They arranged it as a garden and shaded its quiet corners. When the church was finally built it became, in every sense, the glory of the fortification.

The variations of the general layout were many, numbered practically by each individual church. Following is an excerpt from a letter written by a priest after visiting La Purisima Concepcion in San Antonio.

"Entering the building we went up a step from ground level to the tiled floor of the nave, which entered directly from the door to the altar. . . . On our left was a small vaulted room which served as a baptistry and in a similar location, on our right, a balancing room served as a chapel. These formed the basis for the heavy square towers which rose on either side of the entrance facade. . . . Proceeding down the nave past columns of pilasters projecting from the walls we arrived at a crossing. This was an area which directly preceded the chancel or eastern end of the church. From it, on either side, extended arms off the nave proper, the transepts, being the location for secondary altars. . . . Progressing through the crossing, still toward the east, we came up onto the last section of the church, the sanctuary which terminated in the main altar. Here, in this faraway place, was the echo of the cruciform plan scheme of the great European cathedrals, the design being nothing more or less in shape than a great cross . . ."

In eastern Texas the absence of mission ruins attests to the use of perishable materials such as wood, reed, and inferior sun-dried brick. The absence of stone throughout this whole section predestined the establishments to early oblivion. Father Damian Manzanet, visiting at the governor's house in one of the East Texas pueblos around 1700, wrote: "The house is built of stakes thatched over with grass. It is twenty *varas* (about fifty-five feet) high and has no windows, light entering through the door only. . . . Over the door on the inner side is a little superstructure of rafters very prettily arranged . . ." It was from such examples that the missionaries of eastern Texas borrowed their scheme of building.

The presidios of this whole section, built of perishable materials, have disappeared so completely that only in a few instances are their sites remembered. There was till recently one notable exception in the old stone fort at Nacogdoches, erected for the defense of the pueblo of Bucareli which was moved from there to the banks of the Trinity River. But that too fell to the ravages of time. In 1806 the old fort was being used commercially by the firm of Barr and Davenport and thereafter served a variety of uses until its demolition, as warehouse, town hall, tavern, office building, saloon. The present Stone Fort Memorial at Fredonia and Hughes streets in Nacogdoches is partially built from stones of the original building.

In central and southwestern Texas we discover more stable structures. The lack of lumber in these areas was a blessing; the extant Texas missions is our reward. An analysis of the old mission structure reveals that as least seven materials were used in the building materials: adobe, stone, concrete, lime, tile, wood and metal.

An old description of adobe making is worth quoting here: "Given a location where clay was easily removed, its strata being in many cases on the surface, the mission builders first dug a gen-erous-sized pit, stacking the excavated clay by its side. The hole was filled with water possibly brought in leather buckets from a nearby creek. Into this veritable cistern the clay was returned by the shovelful, straw and grass sometimes being added for their binding quality. A great stirring of the mixture went on through this process till the pit was filled with an ooze of thick consistency. Often it was unnecessary to add grass since the natural grit of the finely disintegrated rock in the clay served the binding purpose. Mules and horses were often tethered in the pit, if it were shallow: their manure adding value to the mixture and their hoofs giving it the required violent churning. It was an ingenious if lazy method."

In every section of Texas, excepting the eastern reaches toward the Louisiana line, there is some measure of building stone. The many stream beds near the mission sites presented the missionaries with a supply of rough boulders which were, in many instances, used in their original foundation and walls. This resulted in an irregular sort of cobblestone mass made up of whatever local gran-ite, sandstone, or slate came to hand. These stones were used in connection with adobe, a mixture of the two materials running random through the thickness of the walls. Sometimes stone was quarried from productive pits nearby. Remains of some of these may be seen in fields opposite the mission sites. In several declivities not far from some of the San Antonio missions are signs of the hands of laborers who tugged at rock on the site two hundred years ago. In this area the product was called conception stone, and was very appropriate to the builders' needs. It was a limestone of such nature that it remained fairly soft for some time after removal from the ground. This allowed the pioneer sculptors to work its surface into delicate moldings and fantastic flowers. It did not split under the chisel, and fairly deep undercuttings were possible in its soft thickness. After being set in place and carved in the recess of a portal or the frame of a decorative window, exposure to the air would gradually harden it, so that with the passage of years a surface which had been easily carved became set in a lasting, durable pattern.

The friars, experimenting with adobe, discovered a type of concrete that approached in quality the present-day product. Adobe mixed with pulverized stone, sand, and water accounted for the formula. This was used where stress was not intense. When poured over wooden forms it hardened into great monolithic areas such as the crossing dome of Conception Mission.

Lime abounds in Texas but it is of an inferior quality. The padres, however, refined it by extreme heat and used it in plaster on both interior and exterior surfaces. Also they used it in the mixing of whitewash, which was very popular in the perennial improvement of dark masonry interiors.

The same clay which proved so valuable in making adobe, from which sun-dried bricks were fashioned, also was used in the making of tile and paving brick. The padres first selected a superior type of clay which was kneaded into flattish slabs. To this they added color pigments and molded the pancake blocks around wooden cores. The core was semi-cylindrical in shape and from end to end diminished in diameter as much as two inches, its tapering length being sometimes as much as twenty inches. This shaping allowed the overlapping of one tile upon another as they proceeded up the roof to the ridge. The clay on the mold was slowly baked in low heat until the tile itself was detached from the wooden core. Thereupon it was removed from the oven and its rougher edges and imperfections smoothed off. Finally it was returned to the oven to bake once more at an intense heat for a short period. Glazing was seldom included in the process. Paving brick was manufactured in a like manner and came to replace wood as flooring.

In the preserved missions of Texas, wood is noted only in details. The padres had their choice of live oak, the many nut trees, cedar, and pine. Wood was usually reserved for doors, and the builders resorted to panels of short measurement since the wood in Texas almost never provided great lengths. It was also used, unbarked, for the support to doorway shelters of the residences surrounding the patio, sometimes as lintels above window openings and as short beams from which to suspend the tower bells.

There were no iron sources known in Texas at the time the Franciscans were building missions. The metals used in the decorations of the missions were brought in from Mexico, iron, copper, and silver predominating. Local smiths worked it to the taste of the padres. Door hinges, bolts, grills, and decorative flat studs and scrolls were fashioned on the location. The mission bells were cast abroad or in Mexico, with the exception of the very small ones which the lay craftsmen were able to produce in the pueblos.

It is seen, then, that the architecture of the Texas missions is a blend of European-Spanish-Mexican art, influenced greatly by three unrelated elements: the materials and labor available, the ingenuity of the individual missionaries, and local improvisation. It has been called "ultra Baroque"; it has been described as "rhythmically symmetrical," "exuberantly decorated," "pictorially beautiful"; it is said to possess "vigorous plastic sentiment coupled with clever and artistic use of polychromic effect." It is interesting to note that the Franciscans oriented their churches east and west; and that the most common plan was a long nave crossed at its upper end by a shorter one, thus forming a cross. The outstanding exception to this design is Mission San Jose, near San Antonio; typical of it is Concepcion, also in San Antonio. Of all the Texas missions, San Jose and Concepcion remain in the most perfect state of preservation. Because of their state of preservation, one may draw aside the curtain of time and glimpse, if but briefly, upon the architectural splendor that for centuries held Europe, and with much deep and abiding devotion was brought to the New World by the Franciscan fathers.

7
Chronological Catalogue of Texas Missions

Nuestra Señora de la Guadalupe de El Paso	1659	El Paso, across Rio Grande River
Corpus Christi de la Ysleta	1680–82	Ysleta, near El Paso
Nuestra Senora del Socorro	1681	Socorro, near El Paso
San Lorenzo	1682	El Paso, on Rio Grande River
San Antonio de Senecu	1682	Near El Paso
San Francisco de los Julimes	1683	Near Presidio
San Cristobal	1683	Near Presidio
San Francisco de los Conchos	c. 1683	Near Presidio, across Rio Grande River
El Señor San Jose	1683–84	Near Presidio
La Navidad en Las Cruces	1684	Near Shafter
Apostol Santiago	1684	Near Presidio
San Clemente	1684	Near Ballinger
San Pedro Alcantara	1684	Near Presidio
San Antonio de los Puliques	1684	Near Presidio
Santa Maria la Redonda	1684	Near San Estaban Lake
Mission de la Cibolos	1684	Near Shafter on Cibola Creek
San Francisco de los Tejas	1690	Weches, in Weches Park
Santisimo Nombre de Maria	1690	Near Weches
San Francisco Solano	1699	Rio Grande River, across from Eagle Pass
Nuestra Señora de la Purisima Concepcion	1716	Near Douglass
Nuestra Señora de la Guadalupe de los Nacogdoches	1716	Near Nacogdoches
San Jose de los Nazonis	1716	Near Cushing
San Miguel de Linares de los Adaes	1716	Spanish Lake, near Robeline, Louisiana
Nuestra Señora de las Dolores de Los Ais	1716	San Augustine

San Antonio de Padua	1716	San Antonio
San Antonio de Valero	1718	San Antonio
Mission de las Cabras	1720	Floresville
San Jose y Miguel de Aguayo	1720	San Antonio
San Francisco Xavier de Naxera	1722	San Antonio
Espiritu Santo de Zuniga	1722	Near Port La Vaca
Nuestra Señora de la Purisima de Acuna	1731	San Antonio
San Francisco de la Espada	1731	San Antonio
San Juan Capistrano	1731	San Antonio
San Fernando Cathedral	1734	San Antonio
San Francisco Xavier de Horcasitas	1748	Near Rockdale
San Ildefonso	1749	Near Rockdale
Nuestra Señora de la Candelaria	1749	Near San Gabriel
San Agustin de Laredo a Visita	1749	Near Rio Grande City
San Joaquin del Monte a Visita	1749	Hidalgo
San Francisco Solano de Ampuero	1750	Near Rivilla
La Purisima Concepcion	1750	Near Mier
Santa Cruz Tapaculmes	c. 1750	Near Presidio
Nuestra Señora de Los Dolores	c. 1752	Near Laredo
Nuestra Señora del Rosario	1754	Near Goliad
San Lorenzo	1754	Near Coahuila, Mexico
Nuestra Señora de la Luz	1754	Near Anahuac
Nuestra Señora de Guadalupe	1756	Near New Braunfels
Mission San Saba	1757	Near Menard
San Lorenzo de la Santa Cruz	1762	Camp Woods, Edwards County
Nuestra Señora de la Candelaria del Canon	1762	Near Montell, Uvalde County
Nuestra Señora del Refugio	1792	Refugio

BORDER MISSIONS THAT SERVED AS WAY STATIONS AND ALSO MINISTERED TO TEXAS INDIANS

Santa Rosa	1647	Rio Grande River
San Juan Bautista	1690	Rio Grande River
San Ildefonso	1699	Rio Grande River
Jose de Escandon	1747	Rio Grande River
Reynosa	1749	Rio Grande River
Carmargo	1749	Rio Grande River
Laredo	1749	Rio Grande River
Rivilla	1750	Rio Grande River
Mier	1753	Rio Grande River

8
Missions Classified

THE missions of Texas, for the purpose of this study, are classified into three groups. They are: Missions Lost; Missions Standing; Missions Ruins.

MISSIONS STANDING

MISSIONS RUINS

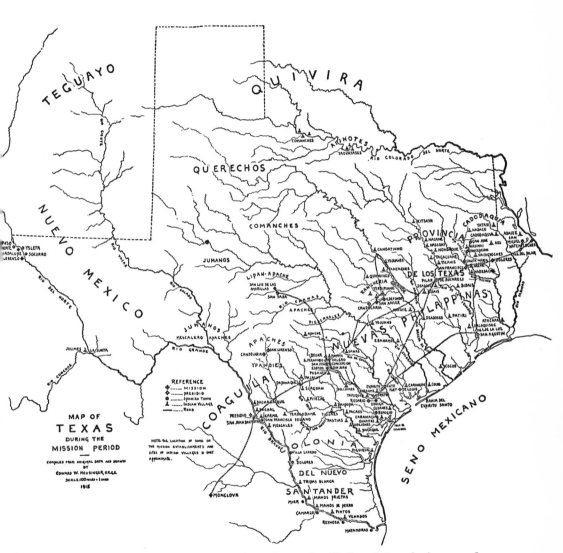

Old map of Texas showing locations of old Spanish missions and presidios.

9
Missions Lost

A thing lost is "that which has perished or been destroyed; no longer to be found . . . gone astray." Unfortunately, most of the missions of old Texas have perished and are no longer to be found. An occasional Texas Highway Department marker has been erected denoting the approximate site where one of the old missions stood. That there is nothing to be found at these sites is understandable when we reflect upon the strife and conflict that Texas has undergone in the past three centuries. Its destiny was carved by hard plainsmen, unenlightened woodsmen, and bold pioneers; not by men of fastidiousness who would pause to admire the architecture of the Old World or to pay homage to the artistic taste of the devoted Franciscans who came and planted missions in this harsh country. Also, the passage of time and the ferocity of the elements, earthquake to tempest, wielded a destroying power. For more than a century the missions were the weed-choked refuge of highwaymen, thoughtless and careless travelers, and wild animals. Vandals ravaged and desecrated their sanctuaries, hammered their great walls; settlers pilfered their sacred stones for barns and dwellings and fences. Many missions in this group were built of perishable materials, such as wood, adobe, and gravel mortar—the East Texas missions. Also in the Missions Lost listing are to be found the temporary missions, which because of extreme hostility of certain Indian tribes or because of internal political reasons were abandoned, some after as short a time as three months; and there were the route stations which served, and with gratifying results, as missions. Regardless of the short duration of some of these missions, once the indomitable and penetrating Franciscan fathers established contact with the natives, the seed of their saintly influence, however limited, was not without its long-range benefit to the final civilizing of Texas.

In colonizing Texas the Spanish military sent expedition after expedition into Texas territory on the king's orders. The purpose of these expeditions was to establish presidios and villas (fortified bastions and settlements) or to recommend locations for later settlement. The missionaries accompanied every expedition. It was their purpose to establish missions, not within the presidios, but near them and under their protection. Often the presidios took their names from the missions, creating some confusion in the minds of many as to the distinction between presidio and mission. Several missions were usually located in the vicinity of one presidio; thus there were nine presidios and over fifty missions established in Texas.

The fundamental desire of the Franciscan fathers was to save souls; and the Church expected them to spread the faith and to win converts. But since the missions were supported by the Spanish king they were expected likewise to serve the king's purpose, which was not only to Christianize the natives but to extend, hold, and civilize the frontiers for the Spanish king. Therefore, as the missions unfold herein, we shall see mission after mission that was founded by the same team of explorers—a Spanish expeditionary force captain and the missionary accompanying the expedition. The founding of a mission sometimes involved more than one priest. The name Father Antonio Margil de Jesus is associated with that of Captain Domingo Ramon and his expedition; Father Nicolas Lopez traveled with Captain Juan Mendoza; Captain Felipe Rabago y Teran and Father Diego Jimenez founded missions together; and Captain Jose de Escandon established them together with one or several of the missionaries accompanying his extensive expedition.

The list of Missions Lost, as noted by the classification drawn previously, comprises by far the greatest number of Texas missions. In this group will be named some missions which will also appear in one of the other groups. A few missions changed their locations, some several times, and in so doing underwent alterations in their names; therefore the delineations, in a few instances, may sound repetitious, but it is hoped that the clarification gained will be worth the seemingly double effort.

Following is a summarized description of the missions included in the Missions Lost category.

Nuestra Señora de la Guadalupe de el Paso was located at Ciudad Juarez across the Rio Grande River from the present city of El Paso. It was established December 8, 1659, by Father Garcia de San Francisco, and dedicated to "the most Holy Virgin of Guadalupe with the above name of El Paso."

The Zuma and Manzo Indians of the area were in the habit of going to the missions in the Spanish provinces below the Rio Grande River to solicit the padres to come to teach and baptize them in their villages. Father San Francisco gathered ten families of Christianized Indians from these missions and took them along to help congregate the Indians of El Paso. With the aid of Indians of the Zuma and Manzo tribes a church and a monastery were built of wood and mud and clay mortar, the insides of which were plastered with lime whitewash. Father San Francisco then planted a cross and held mass. Thus came into being the Mission Nuestra Señora de la Guadalupe de El Paso, the mission that opened the way for the establishment of others in Texas territory. Accordingly, Nuestra de la Guadalupe de el Paso (1659) might correctly be called "Texas' first mission."

Mission San Lorenzo was located on the Rio Grande River about two miles east of Juarez. It was established in 1682 by Father Francisco Ayeta of the College of Zacatecas as a retreat for the refugee Indians from the settlements of New Mexico.

The church was sixty feet deep and twenty-four feet wide. The mission had an early record of prosperity, and as late as 1760 there were thirty Spanish families and twenty-one Indian families living in the settlement. The lands were well cultivated, the orchards produced luxurious fruit, and the vineyards grew excellent grapes. The settlers, however, paid so much attention to their vineyards that they failed to raise enough corn and other staples for their subsistence.

San Antonio de Senecu was located about four miles southeast of present El Paso. It was established in 1682 by Father Francisco Ayeta to accommodate refugee Indians from the Zuma, the Piro, and the Tampiro tribes.

By 1760 there were living at Senecu 111 Piro families with 425 persons; eighteen families of Zuma Indians with fifty-two persons; and twenty-nine Spanish families with 141 persons. They raised corn, wheat, and pumpkins. At times, however, there was a scarcity of grain food and the Indians had to take to the chase and hunt.

The church was larger and better built than many others and therefore was well equipped with all the essentials to minister to the Indians' spiritual needs. It was 100 feet deep and 40 feet wide, and its transept measured 17 feet. It was built of adobe and river bed rock and lime mortar.

San Francisco de los Julimes was located three miles northwest of the present town of Presidio. It was established in 1864 by Father Nicolas Lopez of the College of Zacatecas for the Conchos and Julimes Indians for whom it was named.

In 1683 several deputations of Indian tribes from La Junta (as the junction of the Conchos and the Rio Grande rivers was called) appeared before Dominguez Mendoza, governor of the province, and Father Nicolas Lopez at El Paso to request that missionaries be sent among their people. The leader of this delegation, an Indian called Juan Babeata who had become a Christian at Parral, Mexico, impressed Father Lopez as being not only serious but industrious and enterprising. However, to test him, Father Lopez told Juan Babeata that the Indians could not very well say mass without a church. Juan Babeata took the hint and went immediately and took the measurements of the church at El Paso. Within twenty days a delegation of Indians returned to report that the church had been built. Father Lopez, together with Father Antonio Acevedo and Father Juan Zaveleta, set out at once with the Indians for the new church. They found a commodious edifice of reeds and mud which was equipped with an altar which was an exact replica of the one in the El Paso church.

The mission prospered in its early days, for within a year there were living at Julimes more than one hundred Indians. Subsequent records are missing and there is no clear record of the final years of Mission San Francisco de los Julimes.

Mission San Cristobal, built of logs, river-bed rock and gravel, was located on the banks of the Conchos River near present Presidio. It was founded in 1683 and ministered by missionaries of the College of Zacatecas and was given its name by Juan Trasvina Retis in 1715. There is little history on San Cristobal. However, Captain Mendoza earlier took note of it, chronicling that he halted at a mission called San Cristobal on January 14, 1684. "There were no trees other than mesquite," he wrote, "and the waters of the river were muddy and somewhat alkali."

San Cristobal is recorded to have had a population in 1715 of 180. In 1747 there were 152 people there and in 1760 only 117. It was abandoned after the establishment of Presidio del Norte (the site of the present town of Presidio).

San Francisco de los Conchos was located just across the Rio Grande River from present Presidio, on the west bank of the Conchos River. It was founded c. 1683 by missionaries of the College of Zacatecas.

There is little history of the early years of this mission. It was built of logs and rock held together with river-bed clay. Located in what is today Mexico, it nevertheless served the Texas Indians who traveled that route. When Sergeant Major Juan Antonio de Trasvina Retis, on his expedition of 1715, stopped at the mission he found discipline lax and the Indians in possession of branded stock which obviously belonged elsewhere. He instructed his soldiers not to mention the stolen horses, and promised that the mission would be completely overhauled and ordered Christian instruction to commence immediately.

On June 2, 1715, three masses were said at Mission San Francisco de los Conchos. The third was attended by Trasvina Retis with great pomp, in company of all the Indian chiefs and the principal men of the eight pueblos of La Junta, who had come to the mission to welcome him. There were 380 Indians present and Trasvina Retis was impressed by their intelligence and civil behavior. Father Ramirez, of La Junta, who knew the language of the natives, preached a sermon and reminded the Indians that the padres had come in answer to their request, which he himself had carried to the viceroy. Then Trasvina Retis explained to the Indians that the purpose of his expedition was for their own benefit to make them worthy subjects of the king of Spain, and he told them that two missionaries would be left to minister to them, that the Spanish king would see to their material needs, and that the Indians must take the good word to other tribes to the north. To this the Indians agreed but asked for two more missionaries, alleging that two were not sufficient. They also requested that more missions be established on the other side of the Rio Grande; they especially asked for bells, tools to dig irrigation ditches, and farming equipment. Mission San Francisco de los Conchos was still serving Texas Indians as late as 1760, but by that time the Texas missions were attracting most of the neophytes, Presidio del Norte having been established on the Texas side of the Rio Grande.

Mission el Señor San Jose was located at the junction of the Perdue Creek and Alamito about five miles north of Presidio. It was founded during 1683–1684 by missionaries of the College of Zacatecas and served as one of the La Junta de los Rios pueblo missions. Although established to accommodate Julimes Indians and "those friendly with that nation," it was harassed by Apaches. Since there is no confirming reference available, it is assumed to have fallen victim of the Apache depredations.

La Navidad en Las Cruces was located south of Shafter on Cibolo Creek, exact site unknown. It was established in 1684 at the request of the Jumano Indian, Juan Babeata, who had been baptized in Mexico and had come north to help the Spaniards establish missions and civilize the Texas Indians. It was dedicated in December 1683 by Father Nicolas Lopez. It was a temporary mission and disappeared without leaving a history.

Mission Apostol Santiago was located on Alamito Creek about four miles east of the present town of Presidio. It was formally dedicated on June 12, 1684, by Don Juan Dominguez Mendoza and Father Nicholas Lopez for the benefit of the Julimes and Jumanos Indians.

The mission was built of reeds and timber, but the Indians promised Father Lopez that they would reconstruct it of rock and stone, and requested that four more missions be established for their people of the La Junta country. Father Lopez promised to send the request to his superiors. The governor of Mexico authorized an expedition "for the new discovery of the Jumanos and all other nations who hold friendship with them." He appointed as leader Captain Juan Dominguez Mendoza, an energetic and experienced officer, who, thirty years before, while a young man, had accompanied an early Spanish expedition to the country of the Jumanos. The governor urged upon Mendoza to impress the natives with the respect and love due the king of Spain and the missionaries. When Captain Mendoza reached Apostol Santiago, he called the Indians together and asked them officially if they had ever been visited before this time by Spaniards and whether anyone had ever taken possession of their land for the king. They replied that with the exception of the Franciscan padres no one had ever come to their pueblos. Captain Mendoza then took formal possession of all the La Junta country for the king of Spain. At the same time Captain Mendoza was taking this part of the country for Spain, the Zuma nations who lived to the north between La Junta and El Paso were already in revolt against the Spaniards.

Apostol Santiago proved to be a temporary mission, and after a few successful years it disappeared.

Mission San Clemente was located at the Junction of the Concho and Colorado rivers, approximately fifteen miles southeast of present Ballinger. It was established by the Juan Dominguez Mendoza expedition and dedicated on March 16, 1684, by Father Nicholas Lopez.

San Clemente was a temporary mission built while the Mendoza expedition was camped on the Conchos from March 15 until May 1, 1684. During that time mass was said daily in a rough two-story church constructed hastily of wood and reeds. During this time a number of Indians were baptized by Father Lopez. When the party moved on, Captain Mendoza and Father Lopez promised the Indians that they would return and build a permanent mission on the site. If this was ever done there is no record available.

Mission San Pedro Alcantara was located on Cibolo Creek near Shafter. Its exact site is undetermined. It was founded during 1683–1684 by the Captain Juan Mendoza expedition with Father Nicolas Lopez officiating for the College of Zacatecas.

This mission venture was a bold experiment, for here Captain Mendoza and Father Lopez hoped to Christianize Apache Indians. Little is known of its history except that it was destroyed by the Apaches.

San Antonio de los Puliques was located on the Alamito Creek between Presidio and the Rio Grande River. It was established in 1683 or 1684 by the Captain Juan Dominguez Mendoza expedition and dedicated by Father Nicholas Lopez.

Los Puliques was a temporary mission. A half century later Captain Joseph Idoyaga reported that his soldiers found thirty-six families still living at the ruins of the old mission. Captain Idoyaga tried to prevail on the Indians to rebuild the Los Puliques Mission, but to no avail. At that time the walls still stood intact. Today there is not a trace left, and its site and date of founding are in dispute.

Mission Santa Maria la Redondo was located on the Perdue Creek in the vicinity of San Esteban Lake. It was established by the Captain Dominguez Mendoza expedition in 1684, with Father Nicolas Lopez officiating for the College of Zacatecas.

Captain Mendoza and Father Lopez at this time were busily engaged in the founding of missions in that area under a general order of the viceroy. Upon request of any delegation of Indians in the La Junta country they hastened to establish a mission settlement. Indians of the Natages, the Faraenes, and the Puliques tribes petitioned for a mission and promised to build the church within sixty days. Permission was granted, and when Captain Mendoza sent a delegation at the end of the two months, the church was completed. It was of wood and twigs and with a roof of thatch and mud covered with lime. Like most of the other La Junta missions, this one too disappeared.

Mission de la Cibolos was located in the near vicinity of Shafter, on Cibolo Creek. Cibolo, insofar as mission history is concerned, is little more than a name. It was established by the Captain Dominguez Mendoza expedition and the date is unknown; but since it is known that the Mendoza expedition established several other missions in the vicinity of Cibolo in the early 1680's, it is assumed that the date of its founding is perhaps 1683 or 1684. It was ministered by missionaries of the College of Zacatecas. Father Gregino Osorio was the missionary left in charge.

In 1747, When Captain Joseph Odoyaga and his soldiers visited Mission de la Cibolos they found it in ruins. Indians present told them that it had been razed by Apaches. Since it is known that Apache Indians destroyed other missions near Shafter, it is a reasonable assumption that the Indians told the true story of Mission de la Cibolos.

Mission Santisimo Nombre de Maria was located five miles

northwest of Weches on the Neches River, in Houston County. It was established in June 1690 by Father Francisco Casanas de Jesus Maria (named after himself—Nombre de Maria), under the authority of the College of Zacatecas.

Santisimo Nombre de Maria was the second mission established in eastern Texas. In their early zeal, the priests of Mission San Francisco de los Tejas, the first East Texas mission, sought to extend their missionary work among the Indians of this area, so they moved up the Neches and founded Santisimo Nombre de Maria. Because they were so few in number, and as a result of linguistic difficulties, the padres had little effect on the Indians. Their labors were not a total failure, however. Some Indians, including Chief Xinesi, the head of the Hasinai confederacy, were converted to Christianity at Mission Santisimo Nombre de Maria.

An epidemic of fever broke out among the Indians of the area and the medicine men blamed the disaster on the missionaries. They insisted the holy water was the cause of the epidemic. The Indians at the mission became sulky and unresponsive. The Spanish soldiers left to guard the mission did not help the situation by their disregard for the chastity of the Indian maidens. The future of the mission was already in grave doubt when it was destroyed by a flood. The missionaries gave up the effort and returned to Mission San Francisco de los Tejas.

Mission San Francisco Solano was located on the southern bank of the Rio Grande, across the river from Eagle Pass. It was established by Father Antonio Olivares under the authority of the College of Queretaro, in 1699, for the benefit of Indians of the Pasanac, the Payoyuanes, the Xaranames, the Siguan, the Sibanes tribes.

Because of an insufficiency of water, Mission San Francisco Solano was moved to La Cienga, Mexico, in 1703. Five years later it was removed to San Ildefonso, Mexico, where it remained in existence until 1710; then it was moved back to the Rio Grande and renamed Mission Señor San Jose.

In 1716 Father Olivares asked permission of the viceroy to move the mission to the San Antonio River, where it would be re-established under the San Antonio de Padua mission. In 1718 Mission San Antonio de Padua and Mission San Francisco Solano (Señor San Jose) merged to become Mission San Antonio de Valero, which became the Alamo. (See THE ALAMO, under Missions Ruins, page 140.)

Nuestra Señora de la Purisima Concepcion was first located one and a quarter miles northeast of Mill Creek (known to the Spanish as Los Terreros Creek), six miles south of present Douglass in Nacogdoches County. It was established in 1716 by the Captain Domingo Ramon expedition. Father Isidro Felix de Espinosa, of the College of Queretaro, was placed in charge of the mission.

After being abandoned in 1719 because of the French invasion of Texas, it was re-established by the Marquis de Aguayo on August 16, 1721. Father Gabriel Vergara was named resident priest. It was the only eastern Texas mission not completely ruined during the three years' abandonment.

In 1730, at the request of the missionaries, Mission Nuestra Señora de la Purisima Concepcion was moved to the Colorado River and located in what is today Zilker Park, near Austin, along with missions San Jose de los Nazonis and San Francisco de los Neches. In 1731 the three missions were removed to San Antonio, where Purisima Concepcion was located on the San Antonio River and its name changed to Nuestra Señora de la Purisima Concepcion de Acuna. (See Mission Nuestra Señora de la Purisima Concepcion de Acuna, under Missions Standing, page 107.)

Mission San Jose de los Nazonis was located on a branch of Shawnee Creek about two and a half miles north of the present town of Cushing. The Texas Highway Department has erected a marker on the site designating the location. It was founded in 1716 by the Captain Domingo Ramon expedition, with Father Isidro Felix de Espinosa of the College of Queretaro in charge of the mission. Father Espinosa appointed Father Benito Sanchez as its first resident missionary.

Mission San Jose de los Nazonis was abandoned in 1719 because of the French invasion of East Texas, but was restored by Marquis de Aguayo in 1721. In 1730 it was removed to the Colorado River near Austin and located at Zilker Park along with San Francisco de los Neches and Nuestra Señora de la Purisima Concepcion de los Hainai. The following year, it, with two other missions, was moved to the San Antonio River and re-established as San Juan Capistrano. (See Mission San Juan Capistrano, under Missions Standing, page 88.)

San Miguel de Linares de los Adaes was located on the banks

of Arroyo Hondo, about three miles from Spanish Lake; the site is identified with Robeline, Louisiana. It was founded in 1716 by the Captain Domingo Ramon expedition. Father Antonio Margil de Jesus dedicated the mission for the College of Zacatecas.

Mission San Miguel de Linares de los Adaes was established in the hope that it would deter the French movement westward; therefore its location was the most easterly of all the Texas missions. Little is known of the settlement's early history, except that the project was an ambitious one. The mission was extensive and well fortified, with twenty soldiers in residence for its security. On June 19, 1719, however, the French overran the mission, captured those of its inhabitants who had not already fled, stole its possessions, and stampeded its livestock. As a result of this raid the mission fell into ruins and was destroyed piecemeal by marauding Indians.

The Marquis Aguayo and Father Margil, however, re-established it September 9, 1721, near its former site. The Indians, quite naturally apprehensive, were reluctant to congregate at the mission.

In 1749 there were a "few old Indians too decrepit or lazy to work" residing at the mission. By 1767 Mission San Miguel de Linares de los Adaes was in a state of decay. The Indians "showed little respect for the missionaries, were insolent, and stole the livestock." In 1773 the mission was abandoned and its missionaries, soldiers, and neophytes were sent to San Antonio de Bexar.

San Antonio de Padua was located near the present site of Alamo Plaza in downtown San Antonio. It was authorized by the viceroy of Mexico in 1716, and established in 1718 by Father Antonio de San Buenaventura Oliveras under authority of the College of Queretaro.

Mission San Antonio de Padua's history is synonymous with that of Mission San Antonio de Valero. It was one of the projects that grew out of the interest of Father Oliveras, who had been a member of an expedition under direction of Father Isidro Felix de Espinosa which had entered Texas in 1709. Father Oliveras, a scholarly priest with a keen, inquisitive mind, was impressed by the country around present San Antonio, saw the irrigation potentialities of the San Antonio River waters, and made strong recommendations for missions to be established in that area. So persuasive were Father Oliveras' recommendations that Martin de Alarcon was appointed governor of the district and an impressive expedition was prepared to enter Texas. Almost two years passed, however, before the expedition actually entered Texas.

At San Francisco de Solano Mission, near Presidio San Juan Bautista on the Rio Grande, Father Oliveras gathered Indians to act as interpreters and helpers in the establishment of the San Antonio Mission. Father Oliveras established his new mission on May 1, 1718, and renamed it San Antonio de Valero. He was not disappointed in the Indians he had brought from the Rio Grande. Within one year irrigation ditches had been completed, the engineering of which may be admired even today; fields were planted and herds of sheep, goats, and cattle were flourishing. Therefore it is seen, in a broad understanding, that this Mexican predecessor mission, San Francisco Solano, was considered by many Franciscan students as being linked up with Mission San Antonio de Valero (the Alamo).

In 1724 San Antonio de Valero's site was changed "two gun shots distant." In 1726 it received the neophytes from Mission San Francisco Xavier de Naxera when that mission was discontinued. Its population never exceeded three hundred, yet during the years 1718 until 1761, 1,072 persons were baptized and 454 were married there. Then in 1778 the mission was almost deserted; however, it remained in active service until 1785. Later it became a Spanish pueblo called Señor San Santiago del Alamo. In 1793 the mission records were transferred to the archives of the San Fernando Church. Also in that same year the mission lands were divided among its inhabitants. It eventually became the fortress Alamo. (See Mission San Francisco Xavier de Naxera, following; and Mission San Antonio de Valero, under Missions Ruins, page 121, and The Alamo, under Missions Ruins, page 140.)

San Francisco Xavier de Naxera was located on the San Antonio River two and a half miles south of present-day San Antonio. It was established by the Marquis de Aguayo on March 12, 1722, under the authority of the College of Queretaro.

The year before, when the Marquis de Aguayo was visiting in San Antonio, there came to him a chief of the Ranchero Grande Indians, Juan Rodriguez by name, who asked that a mission be established for his tribe. The Marquis agreed to fulfill Rodriguez' request, and ordered all the Indians of the Ranchero Grande to

retire across the Brazos and assemble at the site proposed for the
new mission. San Francisco Xavier de Naxera continued as a
separate establishment for only four years, enjoying but little success. Then it merged with Mission San Antonio de Valero. Its
structure was of the most primitive type and all traces have long
ago disappeared. Earlier mission historians puzzled considerably
over this mission. Little is recorded that deals with San Francisco
Xavier de Naxera and it was looked upon as something of a
mystery, being listed by several writers as "the lost mission." The
mystery now seems to have dissolved, and it is accepted that San
Francisco Xavier de Naxera is one of the four missions incorporated,
finally, to make up The Alamo. (See Mission San Antonio de Padua,
foregoing; and Mission San Antonio de Valero, under Missions
Ruins, page 121; and The Alamo, under Missions Ruins, page
140.)

San Francisco Xavier de Horcasitas was located two and a half
miles above the juncture of Brushy Creek with the San Gabriel
River on present Kolbs Hill in southwestern Milam County (near
Rockdale). One of the group generally known as the San Xavier
Missions, it was formally established on May 7, 1748, by Father
Mariano Francisco de los Dolores y Viana, who petitioned for
the mission as early as 1745, selected the site, and was the leading
advocate of the mission throughout its existence. Mission San Francisco Xavier de Horcasitas came under the jurisdiction of the College of Queretaro.

Within a year it had a population of 213 Indians. Mission San
Francisco Xavier de Horcasitas had many adverse turns. Bickering
between the Indians and soldiers over liberties taken by the soldiers
with the Indian maidens drove many neophytes away. A year-long
drought added to the mission's misfortunes. Its troubles culminated
in the murder of Father Juan Jose Ganzabal in 1752. Circumstances
of the murder implicated Felipe Rabago y Teran, captain of Presidio San Xavier, and caused most of the remaining Indians and
all but one friar, Father Anda y Altamirano, to flee.

Altamirano remained at San Francisco Xavier de Horcasitas,
keeping the mission in continuous operation until 1755 when Pedro
de Rabago y Teran, without authority, ordered the removal of the
San Xavier missions and Presidio Francisco Xavier to the San Marcos River.

In 1755 San Francisco Xavier de Horcasitas; renamed Mission Nuestra Señora de Guadalupe, was temporarily and unofficially re-established on the Guadalupe River near present New Braunfels.

On January 14, 1757, the properties of all the San Xavier Missions were delivered by the president of the San Antonio missions to Father Alonzo Giraldo de Terreros for the use of the proposed San Saba de la Santa Cruz Mission.

Mission San Ildefonso was located six miles east of San Gabriel in Milam County (near Rockdale). A Texas Highway Department monument marks the site where this mission stood. It was established February 25, 1749, by missionaries from the College of Quere-taro with the hope of Christianizing Indians of the Coco, the May-eye, the Orcoquiza, and related tribes.

Circumstances of the murder of Father Juan Jose Ganzabal, in 1752, and the resulting implication of Felipe Rabago y Teran, captain of Presidio San Francisco Xavier, caused an exodus of the Indian neophytes and friars. An epidemic of smallpox and a long drought added to the mission's troubles. San Ildefonso declined in morale and population, and was finally moved to the San Marcos River. January 14, 1757, the property of all San Xavier missions was delivered to Father Alonzo Giraldo de Terreros for use in the proposed San Saba de la Santa Cruz Mission.

Nuestra Señora de la Candelaria (Our Lady of the Candle-light) was located on the San Gabriel River one and a half miles from the town of San Gabriel, in Milam County. A Texas Highway Department monument marks the approximate site. It was established in April 1749, largely through the efforts of Father Marino Francisco de los Dolores y Viana under authority of the College of Queretaro.

Like the other San Xavier missions, Mission Nuestra Señora de la Candelaria was successful for a time, then began to decline. The causes were many. But the most damaging was the complete lack of cooperation between the missionaries and the military men. The Indians, always sensitive to malice among the Spaniards, reacted sullenly to the strained relations between the padres and the soldiers. They became unruly and indolent; and worse, the behavior was contagious and showed up in its evil effects in the other San Xavier missions.

The beginning of the end for all these missions had its roots in a mass flight of Indians from the Mission Nuestra Señora de la Candelaria and a double murder, which embodied all the ingredients of intrigue and mystery of a modern murder story. Captain Felipe de Rabago y Teran, who had grown distrustful of everybody, prohibited the Coco Indians from entering the stockades armed. When some Cocos went to the mission armed Captain de Rabago y Teran ordered a severe lashing administered. The news of the extreme punishment spread and the entire group of Indians stole away, taking with them their possessions and families. Captain de Rabago y Teran seems to have been looking for an excuse to take revenge on the missionaries. The poor priests had assailed him continually about his soldiers forcing their attentions on the Indian maidens. The captain had only sneered at the padres, for he himself was not without blame in this area of sin.

On the night of May 11, 1752, Father Miguel Pinella and Father Joseph Ganzabal were seated at their humble table in Mission Nuestra Señora de la Candelaria with Juan Joseph Ceballas, who had come to live with the padres. All three were having their evening meal. The heat of the early day had caused them to leave the door of their sultry room open. There came the loud report of a blunderbuss, followed quickly by a second report. The body of the unfortunate Ceballas, who had sought peace in the monastery, slumped across the table, his meal unfinished. Father Ganzabal then did a foolish thing. He took the candle and rushed to the doorway to see whence the shots had come. There was a swish, and an arrow entered the kindly padre's chest and penetrated his heart. Captain de Rabago y Teran quickly blamed the murder on the runaway Cocos Indians. Three days later an Indian named Andres was arrested for implication in the murders. Andres confessed that he had shot Father Ganzabal with an arrow, and that one Martin Gutierrez, a soldier of San Xavier, had fired the blunderbuss that killed Ceballas. However, in his too-detailed confession he had unwittingly implicated Captain de Rabago y Teran by stating that as a runaway Indian he had reported back to the mission two days after the murders and that the Captain had treated him kindly and given him presents. The missionaries now believed that their enemy, Captain de Rabago y Teran, had used the exodus of the Cocos as a cover-up and had instigated the murders, and they pursued the matter among higher authorities. The military did all in its power to defend and clear their captain. Meanwhile, Captain de Rabago y Teran remained in charge of the Presidio and in power over the San Xavier missions and set about to destroy them. He permitted the soldiers utmost license in their conduct with the Indian maidens, and he himself bent every effort to demoralize the community, neutralizing all the good work of the friars. Father Miguel Pinella, after vainly exhorting and admonishing the soldiers and officers to change their course of conduct, excommunicated them all. Troubles only multiplied. Even then neophytes were corrupted by the soldiers. Nothing was left undone to thwart the work of the missionaries. (For the *denouement* of this murder mystery see Nuestra Señora de la Candelaria del Canon, pages 80.)

In the end Captain Rabago y Teran was sent to Presidio San Juan Bautista on the Rio Grande under heavy guard and the padres were vindicated in their work. But it was too late to save the San Xavier missions. Too much evil had already been sowed in the garden of the missionaries. On January 14, 1755, the property of the San Xavier missions was ordered delivered to Father Alonzo Giraldo de Terreros, guardian of the College of Queretaro, for use in missions elsewhere.

San Agustin de Laredo a Visita was located two and a half miles west of Rio Grande City opposite Canargo, Mexico. It was founded March 5, 1749, by Don Jose Escandon and three Franciscan fathers, under authority of the College of Zacatecas. Saint Augustine was chosen as its patron saint.

San Agustin was one of the border missions used as a route station for the Spanish expeditions and padres on their way north. In 1750 Father Juan Bautista Garcia Resuarez was placed in charge, and it was this energetic missionary who made the mission a success. He brought to San Agustin two hundred Indian families and within two years had baptized one hundred fifty-seven. There were twenty-seven Christian marriages.

Floods and epidemics plagued the mission and hindered its continued prosperity. However, when Tienda de Cuervo made an inspection in 1757, he pronounced Mission San Agustin de Laredo a Visita very successful, mainly because the enterprising Father Juan Bautista had paid off the church's indebtedness through a profitable trade in salt.

San Joaquin del Monte a Visita was located at Hidalgo opposite Reynoso, Mexico, on the Rio Grande River. It was established in 1749 by Don Jose de Escandon and Father Fray Marquez, under authority of the College of Zacatecas. Their project was to settle the Rio Grande region.

Escandon supplied the settlers with clothing, tools, seeds, and oxen to till the land and placed Father Agustin Fragozo in charge. Father Fragozo applied himself diligently to his task. By 1752 he had extended his activities to the north bank of the river, grazing the mission's herds of cattle, droves of horses, and flocks of sheep and goats there. The settlement migrated northward a few miles and was called Reynosa. A church was built of brush and mud with a thatched roof. Quarters for missionaries were constructed of the same materials. There were about three hundred Indians under instruction at San Joaquin del Monte a Visita. The natives were docile and friendly, but they had not been formally congregated for lack of food. The location of the settlement had proved ill advised, being subject to floods and incapable of irrigation. A ditch had been opened for the purpose of irrigating the fields but was destroyed by a flood, which nearly claimed the entire settlement. It had been re-dug, but when the river rose it filled up with silt. In 1757 the mission was moved to higher ground and for a time it prospered, having in its most prosperous times ninety-six families with more than three hundred persons living in the settlement.

San Francisco Solano de Ampuero was located three miles north of Rivilla at a settlement called Los Moros. It was established in 1750 under the authority of the College of Zacatecas. San Ignacio Loyola was chosen as its patron saint. Father Miguel de Rivera was the first chosen missionary there but he did not arrive until early in 1751. Meanwhile, the Spanish settlers in the area were duly instructed that they must try to win the friendship and good will of the Indians by all means in their power and that the natives living along both banks of the Rio Grande River should be induced to come and live at the mission.

Between 1750 and 1754, San Francisco Solano de Ampuero was moved three times. First it was removed to a site about twenty miles above its original location. After a year it was moved to a hill in the vicinity of present Guerrero, opposite Zapata, Texas. But this site was unsatisfactory, so it was moved about the end of 1753 to its final permanent location, which is where the town of Guerrero stands today.

La Purisima Concepcion was located about three miles northwest of Roma, in Starr County, opposite Mier, Mexico. it was established in 1750 by the Don Jose de Escandon expedition, and was placed under the supervision of the zealous Father Juan Bautista of the College of Zacatecas.

By 1755 La Purisima Concepcion had twenty-seven families with one hundred sixty-six persons. There were many gentle Indians living with the settlers at Mier for whom they worked, and these regularly went to the mission at Roma for Christian instruction. By 1757 the mission's population had grown to thirty-nine families with two hundred seventy-four persons. Up to this time no regular priest had been assigned to La Purisima Concepcion, and both the settlers and the Indians began to clamor for proper attention for their mission. In 1763, by royal decree, it was ordered that steps be taken to remedy the situation at Roma. Today there is no trace of the successful little mission, but the town of Roma stands on its old site.

Santa Cruz de Tapaculmes was located on the Rio Grande, south of Presidio. It was one of the missions established at La Junta de los Rios under authority of the College of Zacatecas. Early records are not available, and some students place Santa Cruz Tapaculmes on the Mexican side of the Rio Grande. Its exact site is in dispute. The first record of Santa Cruz Tapaculmes indicates that the mission had been operating for many years. At that time, 1789, its population was seventy-six. In 1793 its population was one hundred. As late as 1795 it is known that the mission had a resident friar. In 1800, Mission Santa Cruz de Tapaculmes and the settlers moved to Presidio del Norte.

Nuestra Señora de los Dolores (Our Lady of Sorrows) was located on Blancas Creek about twelve miles southeast of Laredo. It was established by a cattle baron of Coahuila, Jose Visquez Borrego, in accordance with the wishes of Don Jose de Escandon, who sought to colonize the entire lower Rio Grande territory. It was ministered by missionaries from the College of San Fernando.

In 1755 Escandon, in a report to Mexico, expressed regret that there was no regular missionary assigned to Mission Nuestra Señora de los Dolores. Instead, the Indians were being ministered to by one of the padres from Rivilla. Nevertheless, he reported that thirty Indian families were residing there and that they were well instructed.

Two years later, when another inspection was made, there still was no regular missionary at Nuestra Señora de los Dolores. However, it continued in existence for at least five more years, when the viceroy ordered that a priest be sent to the mission or else be abandoned. It was abandoned.

Mission San Lorenzo was located about thirty miles south of the Rio Grande River in Coahuila, Mexico. It was established December 21, 1754, by Don Juan Bustillo y Ceballos and Father Alonzo Giraldo de Terreros.

San Lorenzo was established with the hope of civilizing and Christianizing the Apaches in that district. Little success had been reported from the Texas missions which were trying to tame the Apaches, but since three Apache chiefs from Texas had asked the Franciscan fathers that a mission be established below the Rio Grande River for their people, it was thought that this one might succeed where the others had failed. Three priests labored assiduously at San Lorenzo and with diligent application managed to get some of the Apaches to come to the mission to work and take instruction. But dissatisfaction arose among the Indians and on November 4, 1755, the Apaches attacked the mission and burned its buildings to the ground.

San Lorenzo, though not a Texas mission, can be considered one of the chain of Texas missions linked in the futile attempt to civilize and Christianize the Apache Indians.

Nuestra Señora de la Luz (Our Lady of the Light) was located six miles northwest of present Anahuac, across the bay from Houston in Chambers County. A Texas Highway Department monument was erected to mark the site. This mission, also known as Nuestra Señora de la Luz del Orcoquisac or the Orcoquisac Mission, was established late in 1756 or early 1757 by Franciscan missionaries of the College of Zacatecas in conjunction with Presidio San Agustin de Ahumada.

In 1754, Joseph Blancpain, a French trader, was arrested near the mouth of the Trinity River by Spanish soldiers. As a result of the fears aroused by this encroachment, Governor Jacinto y Juaregui two years later established Nuestra Señora de la Luz Mission near the mouth of the Trinity River for the stated purpose of Christianizing the Indians of the area, but whose real purpose was to affirm Spanish authority in that section of the country. Every effort was exerted, however, by the padres to convert the Indians. The military and the ecclesiastical powers were constantly clashing. The location of the mission was in unhealthy surroundings and as a consequence the soldiers were often sick. In February 1758, Father Joseph Francisco Caro wrote his superiors asking that the mission be moved or abandoned. In 1772 the Marquis Rubi, after an inspection, ordered that the "imaginary mission" be extinguished.

Nuestra Señora de Guadalupe was located on the Guadalupe River at present New Braunfels. It was established in 1756 by Father Mariano Francisco de los Dolores y Viana, under sanction of the College of Queretaro but did not have final approval from the viceroy. Its purpose was to assemble those neophytes of the abandoned mission of San Francisco Xavier de Horcasitas who did not wish to enter Mission San Antonio de Valero. The mission was on a temporary basis, awaiting official approval of its founding, which never came. In January 1757, there were at Mission Nuestra Señora de Guadalupe four Spanish families, two priests, and forty-one Indians, all refugees from Mission San Francisco Xavier de Horcasitas. Mission Nuestra Señora de Guadalupe continued operating until March 1758, when it was ordered abandoned to prevent its possible destruction by the Comanches.

San Lorenzo de la Santa Cruz was located on the east bank of an upper branch of the Nueces River in the valley of San Jose, generally called El Canon, and was at or near present Camp Wood in Edwards County. It was also known as El Canon Mission. It was founded January 23, 1762, by Felipe de Rabago y Teran, Captain of Presidio San Saba, and Father Diego Jimenez, president of the missions of the Rio Grande.

Mission San Lorenzo de la Santa Cruz gathered a number of Lipan-Apache Indians but never received the approval or support of the viceroy. An early cynical account of the mission read: "The little mission of San Lorenzo de la Santa Cruz served only to give employment to a detachment of thirty men and an officer of the presidio of San Saba and to maintain two unprofitable missionaries. It had no other value than to provide a stopping place for the pack trains which enter to supply the presidio."

Nuestra Señora de la Candelaria Del Canon was located on the Nueces River near the present town of Montell in Uvalde County. It was founded February 8, 1762, by Felipe de Rabago y Teran, Captain of the Presidio San Saba, and Father Diego Jimenez.

It will be recalled that Captain Felipe de Rabago y Teran, co-founder of the above mission, was in charge of the Presidio de San Xavier at the time of the murders of Father Joseph Ganzibal and Juan Joseph Ceballos, on the night of May 11, 1752. There was little doubt but that Captain de Rabago y Teran was seriously implicated in the double murder. However, he had, over the years, escaped punishment. The case illuminates the awkward position of the Franciscan friars whenever they came directly in conflict with the Spanish military powers. But the persistent, and in this instance self-righteous, friars would not give up, so strong was their evidence against Captain de Rabago y Teran. Finally he was brought to trial, along with other guilty parties, in San Antonio de Bexar. The wily captain attempted a defense, asserting, as he had originally, that the Coco Indians had killed Father Ganzibal and Ceballos of their own accord. As the trial developed, however, some astounding facts came to light.

It was learned that in the summer of 1751, while Captain de Rabago y Teran was in San Antonio de Bexar recruiting soldiers and settlers, he became intimate with the wife of Ceballos; Ceballos was at that time a citizen of San Antonio de Bexar and had enlisted in the captain's company. By the time the company reached San Saba the brazen liberties that Captain de Rabago y Teran continually took with Ceballos' wife so enraged the husband that he took his grievances to the mission (Nuestra Señora Candelaria) and publicly denounced the captain. The captain, claiming that the man had threatened him, his superior officer, ordered Ceballos flogged and put in chains, and continued his attentions to the prisoner's wife.

Father Ganzabal, one of the priests at the mission, when he learned of Captain de Rabago y Teran's scandalous affair and outrageous cruelty, went to the presidio and protested to the captain, demanding that he end his licentious ways and free the hapless Ceballos. The captain responded with fiendish malice. He had Ceballos securely pinned against the wall of his cell by five spikes, placed a bed before his victim, and made love to his wife in the presence of the helpless prisoner.

This was too much for the outraged Father Ganzabal. He threatened to send a detailed report of the captain's conduct to the College of Queretaro and to the viceroy. To calm the excited priest, Captain de Rabago y Teran delivered the unlucky Ceballos to the mission and promised to send the woman back to San Antonio de Bexar and to mend his own ways. This was only a wily ruse; the captain's hatred for the priests was even greater now that his power had been threatened. And a few days later, while Father Ganzabal and Ceballos were having their frugal meal in the padre's tiny room, Ceballos was shot dead with a blunderbuss and Father Ganzabal was killed with an arrow shot from the darkness. Although the captain tried continually to blame the crime on runaway Indians, the finger of suspicion never left the officer. (See pages 74–75)

There is no record of Captain de Rabago y Teran ever paying for his part in the heinous crime. The military powers, by some incomprehensible reasoning, felt obligated to sustain their establishment against that of the church. Captain de Rabago y Teran continued to command presidios and to establish missions in the new country. So a decade later we find this very able, if criminal, Spanish officer going about the work of colonizing Texas for the king of Spain.

The establishment of Mission Nuestra Señora de la Candelaria was the last attempt to Christianize and civilize the Apache Indians. During the four years of its operation the results were unrewarding. The Indians deserted frequently, returning to the mission only to receive food and gifts. The padres were unable to bring an end to the intertribal warfare. Nuestra Señora de la Candelaria was deserted in 1766 by the neophytes for reasons not recorded. That same year it was abandoned.

Border Missions Serving Texas Indians. Geographically considered, Texas in the seventeenth and eighteenth centuries was a somewhat indefinite and changing entity. The demarcation between

Texas and New Mexico had not been defined; the Rio Grande River, in a general sense only, divided the province of Tejas from Coahuila and other Mexican provinces reaching that river. The Rio Grande River is also known to have shifted the course of its main stream from time to time, changing the locations of several missions.

Old Spanish missions that were established within the boundary of the present state of Texas number fifty-one. In cataloguing these missions, in the name of the consummate, we ought to take into account those border missions which not only played an important role in Christianizing Texas Indians, but also served as valuable way stations for the indomitable Franciscan fathers who, with their worldly belongings on their backs, came trudging into Texas from Mexico. These border missions were all on the lower Rio Grande. They were: Santa Rosa, 1647; San Francisco, 1683; San Juan Bautista, 1699; Jose de Escandon, 1747; Reynosa, 1749; Camargo, 1749; Laredo, 1749; Revilla, 1750; Mier, 1753.

10
Missions Standing

THE Missions Standing group, unfortunately, comprises the shortest list of Texas missions. This classification includes the missions still standing mainly in their former state, or with such minor and expert restoration that their original splendor and beauty has not been disfigured or spoiled by the restorer's brash hand. These missions number five and they are all located in the San Antonio area.

Church of Mission San Francisco de la Espada, near San Antonio.

San Francisco de la Espada Mission, San Antonio, Texas.

They are: San Francisco de la Espada (Pg. 85), San Juan Capistrano (Pg. 88), San Jose y Miguel de Aguayo (Pg. 91), Nuestra Señora de la Purisima Concepcion (Pg. 107), and San Fernando Cathedral (Pg. 110).

SAN FRANCISCO DE LA ESPADA

Mission San Francisco de la Espada was the re-establishment of two missions removed from eastern Texas, San Francisco de los Tejas and San Francisco de los Neches. The new mission, in its final location on the San Antonio River, was dedicated on March 5, 1731, to Saint Francis of Assisi.

One evening in a vision the founder of the Franciscan Order saw himself in a splendid apartment filled with all kinds of arms, rich jewels, and beautiful garments marked with the sign of the cross. In the midst of them stood Christ, who said, "These are the riches reserved for my servants, and the weapons wherewith I arm those who fight in my cause." From this Saint Francis thought that he was to be a great soldier, and it is from this phase of his life that Mission San Francisco de la Espada received its militant name, the translation being "Saint Francis of the Sword."

In 1689, Don de Leon, governor of Coahuila, returning from an unsuccessful expedition to drive out the French colony that La Salle had established on Matagorda Bay, visited the Spanish settlement at San Antonio de Bexar. He was so pleased with the surrounding country and with the attitude of the Indians he saw there that he ordered another mission established. The East Texas missions named above moved there and settled for a time on the Medina River but later changed to another location on the San Antonio River, about eight miles south of present downtown San Antonio. It was established under the authority of the College of Queretaro.

Standing in an undisturbed location in the country, it has survived the encroachment of modern commercialism and its attendant despoliation. The present structure has been partly restored but the front wall remains in its former state of preservation, with its impressive effect. Its openings are framed in smooth-dressed limestone quite light in color, while the rest of its surface has a rough and distinctly Old World texture due to the random use of irregular stone and deep-brown brick. The mission style is one of massive simplicity. The entrance wall embodies the open-gable motif, having its bells suspended in openings at the top of its pyramidal façade. The door is one of definite Moorish flavor.

The plan of the church itself is a diminutive cruciform shape with transepts which are no more than closets off the nave, the length of the whole being about 80 feet. Originally it had a low barrel-vaulted roof of masonry.

Buildings and parts of the old wall still stand nearly on Espada Road. By diligent search in the grass and undergrowth, one can make clear the entire layout of the old mission complex. It was encircled by an irregular-shaped wall, roughly 350 feet square. The foundation had been laid several years before the mission was completed. The builders ran out of stone, and the Indians, being normally indolent and averse to sustained effort, could not be induced to carry the necessary stone blocks over long distances. A quarry, however, was discovered nearby and the work was completed.

The friary, where the missionaries lived, was adjacent to the church and had two stories, with three rooms on the ground floor and two above. There were separate quarters for the workshops and neophytes. Nearby, also, were the kitchen and offices. The granary, like the monastery, was built of stone and mortar and was a large and spacious structure. The Indians were housed in buildings of three tiers arranged around the sides of the wall. Located between these and the church, and projecting into the open fields outside the enclosure, there stands a circular bastion of walls two feet thick. It is solidly built of splintery gray fieldstone, with a diameter of twelve feet. This ancient bunkhouse served as a fortification and sentry post. Instead of windows, there were openings for the muzzles of guns, and at its base there were three openings for cannon, the muzzles commanding the plains beyond. Mission San Francisco de la Espada, in this respect, strongly reminds the visitor of a veritable rampart transplanted from medieval Europe, the feudal castillo of Gothic Spain being its inspiration.

One of the special features of the San Antonio area which attracted Don Alfonzo de Leon and inspired him to ask for more missions to be established there was the feasibility of using the waters of the San Antonio River for irrigation purposes. Irrigation was absolutely necessary to the success of any mission located there, for without it no crops could be raised in that soil and climate; and the products of the field were the principal means used to attract the Indians to the missions and hold them there. Corn, beans, melons, cane, and chili had to be raised for their consumption, and cotton so they could be supplied with clothes.

At the time it was selected, the location for Mission San Francisco de la Espada, as far as the river was concerned, seemed well chosen, for at this point the river was deep and the water swift and clear. But the padres discovered too late in building that the river bed was so low that the water was not available for irrigation. But the difficulties facing those undefeatable friars, instead of causing them to abandon the project, merely elicited from them a display of greater ingenuity and perseverence. Today one can witness the genius of their work. The water had to be drawn from the San Antonio River nearly two miles distant and transported over obstacles that would give pause to modern engineers. Work was begun on the aqueduct in 1740 and completed in 1745. It is still operative, and can be seen to the left of the road about a mile north of the mission.

Being the most exposed of the San Antonio missions, San Francisco de la Espada was subjected to Apache raids. During 1736 and 1737 these savages made frequent raids on the mission, killing the soldiers assigned there and carrying away much stock and many horses. A band of Apaches under the leadership of a chief called Cabellos Colorados raided the mission and stole about forty horses. The soldiers went in pursuit and captured some of the thieves. The Indians, enraged, returned a few days later and surprised and killed two Indian women from nearby Mission San Juan Capistrano, and two more from Mission Concepcion. Shortly afterward they took two little Indian boys from their mothers in plain sight of Espada Mission. The next day five Indian women and two boys from Mission Espada, out gathering fruit on the Medina River, were suddenly attacked by a group of Apaches. They killed the women and horribly desecrated their bodies, slicing their abdomens with fiendish glee, and carried away the boys.

When secularization was completed in 1794, Mission Espada began to deteriorate. As time crumbled the buildings, the mission was used by various wayfarers and adventurers. Texas colonists first encamped there on their way to San Antonio in 1835. Sam Bass, the Texas bandit who was finally ambushed and slain at Round Rock, is said to have used it as a hiding place for money, gold, and jewels taken in stagecoach robberies, and that he had a girl named Judy who used to rendezvous with him there at night.

Church of Mission San Juan Capistrano, near San Antonio.

SAN JUAN CAPISTRANO

San Juan Capistrano was formerly an East Texas mission named San Jose de los Nazonis, located two and a half miles north of the present city of Cushing. The Texas Highway Department has erected a marker designating the exact site. It was first moved to the Colorado River, near Austin, and in 1731 was relocated on the east bank of the San Antonio River, seven miles due east from San Antonio.

The newly established mission was named after Giovanni da Capistrano, born in the Italian Abruzzi in 1386. This Saint John of

Capistrano was a Franciscan friar who, after the capture of Constantinople by the Turks, was sent out to preach a crusade for the defense of Christendom. At the siege of Belgrade when Mohammed was repulsed by the Hungarians, Giovanni was seen with his crucifix in the midst of battle, encouraging and leading the soldiers. In 1690 he was canonized in commemoration of the deliverance of Vienna from the Infidels (1683). His attributes are the crucifix and the standard with the cross.

San Juan Capistrano did not make as much progress as the other San Antonio missions. Its exposed location brought it under frequent Indian attacks, and the lands allotted to the mission were not sufficient for its horses and cattle and the raising of the required crops. The mission owned about one thousand head of cattle and thirty-five hundred sheep and goats. To care for these it had one hundred saddle horses and four hundred mares which were pastured in eleven droves. At one time there were fifty-one families living at the mission, a total of two hundred and three persons of both sexes and all ages. By about 1780 it had begun to decline and its population consistently diminished. It was secularized July 4, 1784.

Today one is able to trace the entire building scheme of Capistrano by means of foundations which vary in height from three inches to six feet and eventually rise to the full heights of the original wall, whose dimensions measured 400 feet by 300 feet. The church itself fell into deterioration early, and meager description has been left the historian. The existing portions, however, show a narrow, simple hall about eighty feet in length on one wall which are pilasters and marred capitals. At one end is a door giving on a small octagonal foundation, which was the baptistry in the base of the tower.

The friary was described as being "composed of four cells, two for the missionaries and the other two for guests, with a corridor connecting two offices, a refectory, kitchen, and workshop rooms. The rooms were small but were built of good mission masonry: irregular river-bed stone alternating with better dressed material, and overlaid with a thick coat of plaster.

The chapel has been largely restored, but its original architecture, a mixture of the Moorish and Romanesque influence, has been preserved to a discernible degree. The design of the chapel entrance and building face is a departure from earlier mission designs in Texas. Above the entrance the two-foot-thick wall climbs in a pyramidal shape. In this are three arched openings, two side by side and one above, wherein bells were suspended. Therefore a bell tower was not required. The motif is called "open gable," and is to be found in latter-day missions in Texas.

The interior of the chapel is an undeveloped long rectangle. On the walls are faint remains of painted decorations. Before restoration work was done on the chapel, these were described by Father Bouchu in the last century:

"A painted rail about four feet high running around the chapel first attracted the eye, then the elaborately painted Roman arch in red and orange over the doorway. The design of this decoration is decidedly of a Moorish caste with corkscrew and tile work, and pillars of red and orange squares. These pillars are about twelve feet high and support another line or rail of color and upon this upper line are a series of figures of musicians each playing a different instrument. The figures are for some reason more indistinct than their instruments, the latter being accurately drawn and easy to distinguish. One of the figures over the frescoed arch of the door is a mandolin player, portions of his chair and instrument being quite plain, done in dark brown and red. To the right of him is a violin player, the best example of them all, the violin bow and features of the face being distinct: his hair is black, his lips red, face and legs orange, feet black, the body of the violin orange and the rest of him and the bow red. To the right of him is a guitar player dressed in a bluish green color, sitting in a red chair. The lower rail, which is much the most elaborate of the two, supports here and there a painted flowerpot and flowers in incongruous colors of bluish green and dull red, carnations being the prime favorites, and with an occasional cross on a pointed pedestal or dado."

From this rather detailed description we can conclude that the paintings were the work of Indian artists of that time. The garish result reminds us of the commingling of Spanish and Indian culture—a Christian and a pagan expression.

It was in this chapel, one account has it, that the Mexican president and dictator, Santa Anna, "married" the child he renamed Leota a dozen days before the battle of the Alamo. His sharp and amorous eyes fell upon her as he rode into the town with his troops, and that night he had her brought to his quarters to make her his mistress. The girl's mother appeared, furious, and demanded that he marry her daughter. Santa Anna already had a wife in Mexico, but the self-styled "Napoleon of the West" was not to be thwarted in his desires. To placate the child's mother he staged a spurious wedding but insisted that it be conducted in the chapel of Capistrano, because of his admiration of the warrior patron Saint John of Capistrano.

Visitors to Mission San Juan Capistrano may, with a little devoted imagination, stand amid its tumbling walls and venerable shadows and hear the trembling voice of the child mistress as she repeated in hushed reverence her vows to the god warrior from Mexico. They may also allow themselves to be carried back to Capistrano's bustling days, when the mission was filled with the sounds of creaking oxcarts and the shrill cries of little red children at their play, the busy ringing of hammers at the blacksmith shop and the forge, the humming of looms and the gentle lilt of Indian maiden's voices as they turned their spinning wheels, the chit-chat of chickens as they foraged for worms in the mission patio, the mellow tones of the mission bells mingled with the rich deep voice of the padre. . . . All these and a hundred other friendly noises are entombed here with the stones of the Franciscans' early Texas.

SAN JOSE y MIGUEL DE AGUAYO

Mission San Jose y Miguel de Aguayo was founded by the saintly Father Antonio Margil de Jesus of the Zacatecan College on February 23, 1720, two years after the establishment of San Antonio de Valero (the Alamo). This was the second mission founded on the San Antonio River and was located five miles southeast of the Alamo. The original mission was not completed until nearly a decade after its establishment. By then a good stone-and-mortar church had been built, with its tower, its transept, and a single nave with vaulted roof. This was not, however, the San Jose y Miguel de Aguayo Mission existing today whose cornerstone was laid in 1768. The original mission, though much more simple, was nevertheless ample to accommodate two thousand persons. In its tower the church had a good chime of bells and in the sacristy it had a fine supply of ornaments and vestments of excellent material and exquisite workmanship. It had many beautifully carved statues

The Rose Window of San Jose, carved by the sculptor Huisar. According to legend, he carved the window for a sweetheart who died before she could join him in the New World.

The Old Aqueduct, San Antonio.

at the main altar and in the two chapels at either end of the transept.

The mission church was dedicated to two patron saints: Saint Joseph and Saint Michael. Saint Joseph is the patron saint of the deathbed and his attributes include the lily, emblem of chastity, and the budded rose in token of the purity of the relation between himself and Mary. A carpenter by trade, he was chosen from among the widowers of Nazareth by the Lord to be the husband of the mother of the Savior. He died eighteen years after the birth of Jesus, and Gabriel "clothed his soul with a robe of brightness and carried it into heaven." He sometimes holds the Infant in his arms and at other times carries the wallet and staff of the pilgrim. Saint Michael, the Archangel, is regarded as the first and mightiest of all the created spirits. He it was whom God commissioned to expel the rebellious angels and Satan from Heaven. His office is believed to be twofold: that of the patron saint of the church on earth and

Mission San Jose de Aguayo, called "The Queen of the Missions." It typifies the beautiful mission architecture of the period, preserving intact many implements and religious articles of more than two centuries ago.

lord of the souls of the dead. Deciding their merits, he presents to God the good and sends the evil and wicked away to torment. The legends relate that Saint Michael appeared to the Virgin Mary to announce to her the time of her death and that he received her soul and bore it to Jesus. As patron of the church militant he is the winged saint with no attribute save the shield and the lance: as conqueror of Satan he stands in armor with his foot upon the evil one. The "de Aguayo" was added to the name of the mission to honor the Marquis de Aguayo who was the generous governor of the province at the time.

Twenty years later, by mid-1800, San Jose had already attained an enviable stage of development and was recognized as the best organized and, perhaps next to the Alamo, best defended of the

five San Antonio missions. In 1768 the dome of the church collapsed in a storm of hurricane ferocity. The foundation had been
undermined by treasure hunters digging at its base and so the
present church was begun. Its mission design is superb, its architectural scope unsurpassed in Texas missions. It encompasses a
blend of the Gothic, the Moorish, and Romanesque influence,
decorated in Renaissance artistry.

When Father Juan Morfi, a Franciscan historian, visited the
mission in 1777 he said of it: "The convent, or living quarters for
the missionaries, has two stories with spacious galleries. The one
on the second floor opens out on the flat roofs of the Indian
quarters and is very convenient. Two quadrants [sun dials] on
vertical columns were set up there; they were made out of a species
of limestone so soft that when first brought from the quarry it can
be planed like wood, but which, when exposed to the air, hardens
and can be polished like marble. The figures of the façade of the
church, the bannisters of the stairway of the convent, and the
image of Saint Joseph that is on the pedestal, all were made more
beautiful by the ease with which the stone is worked. There are
enough rooms for the missionaries and for the convenience of a few
guests, as well as the necessary offices for the religious, a large and
well-ordered kitchen, a comfortable refectory, and a pantry. There
is an armory, where the guns, bows and arrows, and lances are
kept, with which to arm the neophytes in case of attack or to act as
auxiliary troops on a campaign, in which case the mission provides
them not only with arms and ammunition but with supplies as well.
In a separate room are kept the decorations and dress with which
the Indians bedeck themselves for their dances, so they will forget
their native *mitoties* [pagan festivities]."

The soldiers' quarters, where the mission guards lived, were
opposite the church. There was the granary, space for the carpenter
shop, the spinning and weaving rooms, and other necessary cells.
There was also a place where sugarcane was made into molasses
and brown sugar, the first record of sugar being made from sugarcane in Texas. The whole area was surrounded by a strongly constructed wall roughly in the shape of a square. Arranged along
this, on the inside, were the stone quarters where the neophytes
lived. They had flat roofs and loopholes from which to fire upon
the enemy when attacked. Each house had a bedroom and a

Mission San Jose, San Antonio.

kitchen, and each family was supplied with a cooking flatiron (for frying tortillas), a grindstone for corn, a water jar, a bed, a chest of drawers, and a clothes closet. Located conveniently near the houses were several baking ovens. Everything was arranged for the comfort of the new Christians. At this modern mission another first for Texas was achieved, the wonders of which would have startled the cattle barons of a much later era. There was a swimming pool for the neophytes. The water was brought from the river by means of a gravity canal that flowed along the houses, from there into the pool, and out into the adjoining fields, where it was not wasted but used for irrigation purposes. Near the soldiers' quarters there was a second swimming pool, an early precedent for segregation practices.

A high degree of civilization was attained by the Indians of Mission San Jose y Miguel de Aguayo. The neophytes were well dressed, had an ample supply of food, and each performed his task willingly. There was a minimum of soldier abuse of the Indian

Dwelling in old walls of San Jose Mission.

maidens; all residents at this mission, Spanish and Indian, lived in a fair state of harmony and enjoyed a prosperous and contented life.

The fields under cultivation were extensive, covering several miles, all being stone-fenced and irrigated by a large canal, dug by the neophytes, and in which fishing was actually done by the Indians and padres. Beyond the orchards and well-watered fields (thanks to the natural springs around San Antonio which made irrigation prosperous and easy) the mission had its ranch, at which it ran several thousand head of cattle, droves of mares and asses, sheep and goats in the hundreds of heads. Supplies were furnished by San Jose not only to the presidio of San Antonio but to those of La Bahia, Orocaquisas, and Los Adaes.

The church of Mission San Jose y Miguel de Aguayo is famous for its superb architecture and artistry. The wavering line of the sacristy parapet and the carved spouts which carry rain water off

Interior of Mission San Jose church.

Arches in ruins—San Jose Mission.

Plaque—San Jose Mission site.

its stone and concrete dome are examples of the artistic delicacy of imagination the Franciscan fathers were capable of. They were also men of architectural skill, good workmanship, and artistic ingenuity; and the procuring of such large amounts of building material, at a time when transportation and construction were crude, testifies to their remarkable assiduity and enterprise.

The two staircases leading to the tower are but one illustration of the ingenuity of the missionaries. A winding stairway leads to the second story of the tower. It is enclosed within a circular wall, placed in the angle made by this tower and the south wall of the church. Each step of this remarkable stairway is a triangular block of oaks, hewn by the missionaries and their Indian helpers with singular care, considering the crude tools at their command. From the second story of the tower to the lookout windows in the chamber above, the workers somehow set up the trunk of an immense tree and notched steps eighteen inches wide into it. Crown-

A row of workshop buildings inside the walls of San Jose Mission.

ing all else, perhaps, is the famous Rose Window and the church façade. It has been said that, coming upon this arrestingly beautiful entrance, here the tour de force of all American mission architecture greets the eye. Centered on the façade, which is otherwise free of sculptured ornament, is this great panel, twenty feet wide and extending from ground to roof, pierced with the doorway itself and a generous window above it. Here is all the grace of the Renaissance translated by provincial native tastes into bizarre, tumultuous effulgence of decoration. The concentration of sculpture gives the impression of a perfect unity.

The old mission has its legends, two of which should be noted here. Pedro Huizar, descendant of the architect who designed the world-famous Alhambra, a Moorish stronghold in Spain, was the handsome young artist working on the façade. He was devotedly in love with a girl in his homeland, named Rosa, and she had

San Jose Mission—the old Tower.

Entrance of the chapel inside San Jose Mission.

promised to come to Texas and be his bride. Just before she was due to arrive the last design was carved in the façade. Soon now he would proudly show his work to Rosa and they would be married in the church. The sun was only a few hours old next morning when a rider was seen galloping toward the mission. He placed a letter in the young artist's hand. The ship bringing Rosa was lost at sea; no one had been saved. Huizar's grief seemed almost unbearable. Now only did he realize how much he loved Rosa. Losing her, he felt that his life's work was to bring her beauty to the mission. He would carve a portal for the church that would be the most beautiful in all the New World. He began work on the famous Rose Window, carving rose after rose, all the while dreaming of his lost love. As the years passed his health failed, and it was by sheer force of will that he was able to finish his dedication. It is said that when he had carved the last rose in the window, Huizar felt Rosa's breath on his cheek and heard her gentle voice pronounce his name . . . "Pedro . . ." Shortly thereafter he died, and was buried in the patio under the Rose Window.

Perhaps the saddest and most romantic of the legends about the San Jose y Miguel de Aguayo Mission concerns a young Spanish nobleman, Don Louis Angel de Leon, and his fiancée, Teresa. Desiring adventure, Don Louis traveled to the New World and came to San Jose with one of the missionaries, a kinsman. Just before he was to begin the journey home to wed Teresa, he was killed in a battle with the Apaches and was buried in the mission. The unhappy news was carried to his Castilian sweetheart by his kinsman. As the weeks passed and Teresa found no consolation for her grief, she begged to be allowed to return with the Padre to the mission where her beloved had met his death. However, permission was denied. About the same time, the mission bells for San Jose were to be cast in the town where Teresa lived. In the throng which had gathered to watch the casting of the bells stood a pale, dark-eyed girl. A few curious strangers watched her slip a ring from her left finger and a golden cross from her necklace. Suddenly, in the molten mass, there fell a ring and a golden cross. Many turned their eyes on a dark head bowed in prayer. Those who recognized her also removed their jewels and, throwing them into the furnace, knelt in tribute to this maiden. The day the bells rang out for the first time over the plains around San Jose Mission, a Castilian girl far away in a castle turned her eyes west where the sun sank in a great ball of golden splendor. She prayed that the bells would take a message of love to Don Louis.

San Jose has its "mystery" also. There is the question of the underground chamber and a receptacle which, in recent years, was located where the mill by all rights should have been. It is a circular well-like structure about twelve feet deep. Faint signs of coloring on the walls were found, and at the bottom there was an opening which had been closed with masonry. The walls of the underground room were glazed and plastered, and the ceiling constructed of tufa rock, the floor of flagstone. The arch was described with lines, the centerpoints of which were geometrically accurate. What did the padres use it for—wine cellar, a turbine room, a well, a powder plant, a treasure room? Could it have been used as a torture chamber? Its purpose has never been explained.

The early records of San Jose y Miguel mission have been lost. The padres always kept close and strict records of births, baptisms, marriages, and deaths. The first book of records begins at San Jose with September 1777 and extends to 1884. The first entry is number 831, suggesting that at least one earlier book had existed. The search for this book goes on; lucky is he who turns it up.

In 1792, San Jose y Miguel Mission was secularized and its administration taken from the Franciscans. The Indians lingered and finally abandoned the mission, after which it began to deteriorate. From 1808 to 1835 it was used as a rendezvous for bandits, highwaymen, cattle thieves and robbers; it also served as living quarters for wayfarers. From 1835 to 1844 it was used as a barracks by Santa Anna's soldiers and also for those of the Republic of Texas. After Texas was annexed to the United States, American soldiers were quartered there. During the Civil War the mission was used to hide runaway Negro slaves. Since the days of abandonment there have been tourists visiting the convent who have done more damage to the buildings by chiseling their names in the rare stones and chipping souvenirs from the carvings than all the robbers, thieves, bandits, and soldiers of early times.

The church is seen today in a restored condition, yet the clumsy restorer's hands have not dimmed the original glory of San Jose. It stands as a preeminent monument to the great inspirations of the Franciscan Fathers.

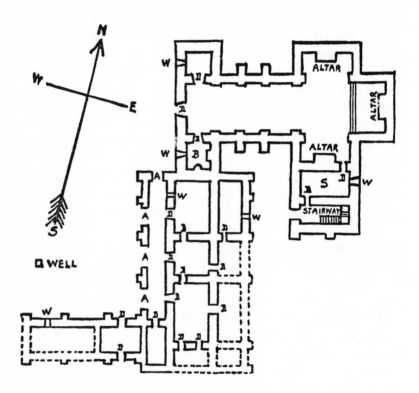

CHURCH AND MONASTERY
MISSION NUESTRA SENORA DE LA PURISIMA
CONCEPCION

References: Solid lines show existing works; dotted lines show ruins. A = arch; D = door; W = window. B is the baptismal chamber; S, the sacristy. The San Antonio River is about one-quarter mile west.

Plot plan of Nuestra Señora de la Purisima Concepcion.

Mission La Purisima Concepcion de Acuna, founded in East Texas in 1716 and moved to San Antonio in 1731. It shares with the Alamo the distinction of having been used as a fort during the war for Texas independence.

NUESTRA SEÑORA DE LA PURISIMA CONCEPCION

Nuestra Señora de la Purisima Concepcion, orignally founded in eastern Texas in 1716, was moved to San Antonio in 1730 and located about two and one half miles south of Mission San Antonio de Valero (the Alamo). It was erected on the site where the "lost mission" of San Francisco Xavier stood before it was moved to join Valero to become one of the four missions which the Alamo, in its checkered history, absorbed.

Remains of the original edifice can be traced by a careful observer. Although the mission began its operation in 1731, the church was seventeen years a-building. In 1745, Father Ortiz visited Nuestra Señora de la Purisima Concepcion and reported: "At this time a fine new church was being built of carved stone and mortar. In the meantime services were being held in a large adobe hall with a terrace roof." He reported that the church was "very pretty," its nave was about one hundred feet by twenty-four feet, and that it was built on the cruciform plan. Its dome had been completed and bells had been installed in its two towers. "Above the main altar there was a fresco of the Cino Señores. Its taber-nacle was gilded, and over the main altar, in an oval-shaped niche, was an elegantly sculptured image in honor of Our Lady of Sor-rows and Our Lady of Pilar. It was furnished with two confes-sionals, several benches and a pulpit. Beneath the two towers there were two small chapels, one dedicated to Saint Michael, with a very pleasing altar, and the other used as a baptistry. Here there was a baptismal font of copper with its cover, three anointers, and a silver shell."

The church stands today practically unscathed by the passage of time and without disfigurement by the hand of the restorer. The sole restoration of Nuestra Señora de la Purisima Concepcion was done by Bishop Nerez in 1887 and consisted mostly of cleaning out the bat guano and whitewashing walls. The architecture is severely plain, though massive and imposing, and one senses faint inspiration of the Moorish intermingled with the Romanesque. The nave is divided into four vaulted bays, looking somewhat bril-liantly clean (perhaps because of Bishop Nerez's handiwork). There are thick loads of masonry, over which is laid a smooth coat of plaster. Down the nave's length there are projections of three pilasters on either side; and upon the capitals of the pilasters rest the transverse arches of the vaults, evidence of the Romanesque system of construction. The "orderly and beautifully gilded" walls Father Ortiz noted in 1745 are today faded outlines of red and orange colors, and the floral and geometric patterns are seen as tones of yellow, buff, dull red, and faded blue, mere ghosts of their former brilliance. The Indian neophyte, on first entering there, must have stood aghast at the tabernacle's striking color and bril-liance. The work was undoubtedly done by Indian artists under the direction of the padres. Paint was made by mixing pulverized field rock with milk, salt, and cactus juice. The coloring depended on the kind of rock and mixture: blue by mixing indigo and char-coal and milk; red and yellow by pulverizing field rocks of that color.

Viewing the church from the front, one is impressed by its

appearance of "massive strength." It is a balanced and impressive façade, giving one an idea of what the completed Alamo might have resembled, since the plans of these two churches are so similar. At Nuestra Señora de la Purisima Concepcion the door itself is about six feet wide and ten feet tall, topped with a geometric three-sided arch, indicative of the Trinity. Twisted over the arch of the door and down along its sides is a carved rope, knotted and looped in a decorative fashion, representing the *cordelier* or simple girdle of the Franciscan friars. This rope has been interpreted as the scourge, or flagellum, usually occurring in representation of the crucifixion. Over the door, in a small scroll, reading from left to right, a Spanish motto is inscribed concerning La Purisima Concepcion, the patroness to whom the church is dedicated. Translated, the words tell us:

"With These Arms Be Mindful of the Mission's Patroness and Princess, and Defend the State of Her Purity."

The entire mission, as was always done, was encompassed by a wall, traces of which remain. It had its friary with necessary cells for the missionaries and other rooms for offices and storage; it was of one story with a pleasing archway along the side. Adjoining the living quarters of the missionaries were the rooms for the looms and workshops. The granary was in a separate building, and had a capacity of sixteen hundred bushels of corn and one hundred bushels of beans. The quarters for the Indians were arranged in two tiers of stone houses on either side of the church and monastery. Each house was decorated with good taste and provided with the necessary pots and pans, its grindstone for corn, and flatiron for cooking tortillas over the coals. The mission's fields were fenced and irrigated by a ditch that led the water from the river, where a stone dam had been built. The ranch had several houses for the caretakers who looked after the herds of cattle, the sheep and the goats.

It was at Nuestra Señora de la Purisima Concepcion that on October 28, 1835, Colonel James Bowie and Captain J. W. Fannin, with ninety Texans were surprised by a detachment of the Mexican army consisting of four hundred men, which surrounded them. A fierce encounter ensued, but the Mexicans were defeated and fled to San Antonio. The Texans lost only one man, Robert Anderson. This, claimed Bowie, was a good omen. Here, at Mission Concepcion, the Texans had won their first fight with the Mexican troops.

SAN FERNANDO CATHEDRAL

San Fernando Cathedral is located in the heart of what today is San Antonio's commercial center. The original church has the distinction of being the oldest parish building in the state of Texas. It was erected on the Plaza de los Islas (now Main Plaza). The church was dedicated and its cornerstone actually laid on May 13, 1734. Before the formal laying of the cornerstone those in charge took steps to have the new building officially designated as the parochial church, and to have the patron saint under whose advocation it was established approved by the vicar, Ecclesiastic Judge, and the curate, who was Bachiller Juan Rocio de Leon. In a public statement, the curate solemnly declared, "In the exercise of my ecclesiastical jurisdiction I pronounce the said building, the parish church of the royal presidio of San Antonio de Bexar, under the advocation of Our Lady of Candlemas and Our Lady of Guadalupe, whom I humbly beg to look upon this new house with pious eyes, taking it under her protection and care." He explained that it was most fitting that the new church should be dedicated to the Blessed Virgin because Saint Anthony had the patronage of the presidio and Saint Ferdinand that of the settlement.

The San Fernando Cathedral one sees today is by no means the original edifice. In its pristine days, San Francisco Cathedral shared greatly in mission characteristics. It was here that the Canary Islanders congregated when they first arrived. It was ideally located for this purpose; its rear gave on the Plaza de Armies (Military Plaza), where the military government had its headquarters. On either side of it was the First Catholic Cemetery. This was later moved to a site that now fronts Santa Rosa Hospital, and later was transferred to Alazan. The only part of the original church that remains is the rear section which fronts the city hall. This is in a good state of preservation. Its massive octagon-shaped walls and the lavish detailing of its beautiful dome identifies its architecture as being of a modified French Gothic style.

When the Canary Island settlers saw the orderly fashion in which the San Antonio missions were run with Indian workers, they conceived the idea of utilizing the mission Indians to work their farms. Governor Carlos de Lugo Franquis, during his short and tempestuous administration, attempted to force the missionaries to supply neophytes to work for the settlers. He went so far as to try to prove that the mission Indians were being mistreated by the missionaries and soldiers assigned to the missions to their protection. He contended that the neophytes would be better treated if allowed to work for wages in the outside. He appealed to the viceroy in Mexico for authority to put his plan into action, but the request was refused.

The old San Fernando Church saw many interesting and exciting scenes enacted on the Main Plaza it faced. There in 1749, the Spaniards celebrated their peace with the Apache nation. Four chiefs in full paint and feathers danced around a hole dug in the center of the plaza. In it were a live horse, a tomahawk, a lance, and six arrows. The chiefs danced holding hands with the Spanish officers and with the Franciscan missionaries; then the horse was buried along with the tomahawk and lance and arrows.

Here, in 1789, six Apache braves, determined to assassinate the governor of the Texas province, forced their way into the Royal House and were cut down by the guards.

Into these same offices, in 1813, strode Bernardo Gutierrez to announce the murder of the Spanish governors of Salcedo and Herrera by his men, in a futile revolutionary attempt to seize Texas and found an independent nation for himself.

On this plaza (and north of it) in 1835, was fought the bloodiest battle of the siege of San Antonio. In the middle of the plaza, in 1836, Davy Crockett, the Tennessee congressman and fighter, stood on a box and made a speech, in which he asked to become a private soldier in "our common cause."

At the west corner on the north side, General Santa Anna, president and dictator of Mexico, maintained an office.

In 1840, thirty-three Comanches, who had come to parley over captives, screamed betrayal when the whites tried to hold them as hostages, drew their bows and arrows, and killed seven Texans before they could be shot to death.

In this plaza Governor Sam Houston, in 1860, delivered his tempestuous orations, crusading to keep the state within the Union.

Here it was that General D. E. Twiggs surrendered the United States troops to the Confederacy. And in a hotel, then on the south side, a little later that day, Robert E. Lee paced the floor all night, arriving at a historic decision.

But perhaps the most dramatic of all scenes the old cathedral ever saw was when on that fatal Sunday dawn, March 6, 1836,

General Santa Anna hobbled to the roof of San Fernando and fired the shot that began the final assault on the Alamo. It was from the church's dome that his red flag, signaling "no mercy for the besieged," had fluttered for thirteen days plainly to be seen by the hundred and eighty-three men besieged in the old mission.

In 1863 it was decided to enlarge the San Fernando Church and convert it into a cathedral for the diocese. The old front was torn away and the present face erected; but a wrangle over finances delayed its completion and for a long time it remained an ugly half-finished eyesore. When finally the work was resumed, a second tower was added, and a new belfry with a set of beautifully attuned bells were installed. The façade was materially improved, with statues of San Antonio's saints placed in its chapel.

San Antonio is unique among Catholic cities in having two patron saints. One is Saint Anthony of Padua, after whom Captain Domingo Teran named the settlement for his arrival at the site on that saint's day. He is the patron saint of children and animals. The other is Saint Ferdinand of Castile who, as Don Fernando III, chartered the city, and after whom it once was called San Fernando de Bejar. This Ferdinand was a great king, warrior, and saint. He died as a penitent with a cord around his neck and a crucifix in his hand.

One of the treasures of San Fernando Cathedral is the hand-carved pulpit, which was rescued from Mission San Jose y Miguel de Aguayo. There are some interesting altars in memory of distinguished citizens of early San Antonio.

Colonel Gonzolez, whom General Houston ordered to gather the bones of the heroes of the Alamo after Santa Anna had them burned, is said to have buried them in San Fernando, but all efforts to locate them have failed. Gonzolez admits gathering and depositing them in several coffins, but in his old age he told conflicting accounts of where he had placed them. There is, however, a crypt on the extreme right of the entrance, purported to contain the bones of Colonel James Bowie, Colonel William Travis, David Crockett, and James Bonham. These bones, when first discovered, were on display in the church for one year before being placed in the white marble crypt.

11
Missions Ruins

THE Missions Ruins group includes those whose foundations are standing or have disintegrated or fallen and may still be traced, and those that have been restored. Also in this list are the missions whose former sites or ruins have given rise to new missions or churches or upon whose locations and ruins towns have been built. Some readers may be dismayed that the Alamo has been placed in the Missions Ruins classification. The Alamo "mission" in downtown San Antonio is not, in fact, Mission San Antonio de Valero but a reconstructed fortress, which even itself is indeed a spurious replica of the original Alamo fortress. The Alamo qualifies for its grouping in Missions Ruins on the grounds that it is a restoration built upon the foundations of a former mission. Notwithstanding the perhaps uncomplimentary and too humble classification of the Alamo in this work, it does receive its full share of honor and glory as, indeed, it truly deserves.

Following are the missions qualifying for the classification Missions Ruins:

Corpus Christi de la Ysleta
Nuestra Señora del Socorro
San Francisco de los Tejas
Nuestra Señora de la Guadalupe de los Nacogdoches
Nuestra Señora de los Dolores de los Ais
San Antonio de Valero
Mission de las Cabras
Espiritu Santo de Zuniga
Nuestra Señora del Rosario
Presidio la Bahia (in relation to Espiritu Santo de Zuniga and
    Nuestra Señora del Rosario)
Mission San Saba
Nuestra Señora del Refugio
The Alamo (San Antonio de Valero)

The restored Isleta Mission in suburban El Paso. The original was founded in 1682. This mission is the center of activities of the Tiqua tribe of Indians who still live in this oldest Texas community.

CORPUS CHRISTI DE LA YSLETA

Although today a modern church commemorates a site of the mission Corpus Christi de la Ysleta, when founded in 1682 it was estimated to have been about four miles southeast of present Juarez. In 1726 and again in 1766 it was reported to be located on the northeast side of the Rio Grande River. These changes in its location are probably explained by the shifting of the main current of the river. Today the settlement of Ysleta, Texas, is built on the old mission's site. Mission Ysleta was founded by Father Francisco Ayeta of the College of Queretaro. It was initially called San Antonio de la Isleta; and was also known as Corpus Christi de la Isleta, and at various times as San Lorenzo del Realito, Nuestra Señora del Carmen, and San Antonio de los Tiguas. Founded for the purpose of converting the refugee Indians fleeing from the Apaches of New Mexico territory, it was used also as a way station for Spaniards traveling from Mexico over the Northern Pass into Texas territory.

With all its numerous titles, little remains of the original church. On May 15, 1907, its existing buildings were destroyed by fire. It had an oddly shaped hipped gable and a tower of three stages with a double belfry and an egg-shaped dome. It was ornamental and its style was probably a blend of Moorish and Romanesque. From the remains of the foundations we know that the church was 145 feet long and 18 feet wide, with a transept that measured 30 feet. It was constructed of masonry made of river-bed rock, gravel, and mortar, and it was composed of "unusual amounts of wooden supplements."

Corpus Christi de la Ysleta had its ranch and fields and orchards. There were extensive vineyards where excellent wines were made, as well as strong brandies. But the inhabitants had many difficulties to contend with, chiefly the river. A dam built across it caused the water to flow into irrigation ditches. The periodic floods frequently caused the dam to wash away. The settlers rebuilt it by making large cylindrical baskets out of willow wands and slender twigs. These they filled with small stones and gravel, and when the flood subsided they rolled them into position.

In connection with Corpus Christi de la Ysleta, it is appropriate here to relate the story of the legendary "Woman in Blue." One hot day in July, 1629, a strange delegation of Jumano Indians from the heart of Texas territory trekked nearly a thousand miles to Mission San Antonio de la Isleta, which was located south of present Albuquerque, New Mexico, to ask in the name of a mysterious Woman in Blue for instruction in the ways of Christianity. The sons of the compassionate Saint Francis, who loved all things because God created them and to whom a soul saved was more precious than gold, jewels, or worldly kingdoms, knew not a day of rest until the call was answered. For years the appeal of the Jumanos haunted them; their desire to visit the distant land where the Woman in Blue had miraculously appeared to the natives became an obsession. They bided their time and awaited the hour. It came many years later, and when it did, time had not altered the desires nor dampened the zeal of the Little Brothers. It is interesting to note that the first Texas mission ministered to the Jumano Indians, and was called by the padres San Antonio de la Isleta, after the New Mexico mission where the delegation of Jumanos first appeared with their story of the beautiful Woman in Blue.

The Woman in Blue has subsequently been identified with Mother Maria Jesus de Agreda, abbess of a famous convent in Spain, who declared that she had converted these tribes during a visit to America in ecstasy.

Ysleta (1682) is said by mission historians to be "Texas's oldest mission." But is it? *Nuestra Senora de la Guadalupe de el Paso* was established December 8, 1659, just south of present El Paso, and north of the location of the original Mission Ysleta. (See Mission Nuestra Senora de la Guadalupe de el Paso, under Missions Lost, page 62.)

NUESTRA SEÑORA DEL SOCORRO

Nuestra Señora del Socorro was located about eight miles south of present El Paso, on the Mexican side of the Rio Grande River. It was founded in 1682 by Franciscan missionaries of the College of Queretaro for the benefit of the Prio, the Tano, and the Jemez tribes of Indians, refugees from New Mexico.

In 1683, because of an Indian uprising, it was moved to a site about a mile and half from Ysleta, Texas. For the next fifty years little is known of Nuestra Señora del Socorro, except that it underwent several changes in name: San Miguel de Socorro; Purisima Concepcion del Socorro; and Socorro del Sur. In 1744 its population included several Spanish families and about sixty Indians. In 1756 it was secularized, its property being distributed among the Indians and settlers. A flood early in the nineteenth century did considerable damage to the settlement. The present village of Socorro, in El Paso County, was built upon its ruins. Today a modern mission, commemorate of the early Franciscan edifice, stands upon the site.

SAN FRANCISCO DE LOS TEJAS

Mission San Francisco de los Tejas was located on San Pedro Creek just northwest of present Weches, in Weches Park. The first mission to be established in eastern Texas (May 25, 1690), it was founded by Captain Alonzo de Leon and Father Damian Massanet.

Restored Mission of San Francisco de las Tejas.

It had three different locations and three names before it finally came to rest on the San Antonio River March 5, 1731. It still stands today in San Antonio, as San Francisco de la Espada, called Mission Espada (the Sword).

San Francisco de los Tejas was the fulfillment of a promise Father Massanet on a previous visit had made the Tejas Indians to establish a mission in their midst. On May 22, 1690, the De Leon expedition reached the first of the Tejas Indians and was cordially welcomed. The Indians proved their sincerity by helping the Spaniards build the mission. The church was completed and officially blessed June 1, 1690. At that time a governor was selected from among the Indian chiefs to organize civil affairs of the neophytes. Four Franciscan padres were left in charge of the mission, with eight soldiers as a security force.

San Francisco de los Tejas fell on hard times. Two successive years floods destroyed the crops and supplies from Mexico failed to arrive. The padres were unable to induce the Indians to live in the stockade. The chief who had been elected governor, and who was to be an example to the other Indians, became surly and untractable. The missionaries grew discouraged and two of them left to work elsewhere.

In October, 1693, news was received in the mission that a plot to massacre the Spaniards had been hatched between the French and the natives of the area. On October 25, after having buried the most prized possessions, the padres and the soldiers set fire to the buildings and slipped away. (It should be borne in mind when considering eastern Texas missions that there is no indigenous masonry in east Texas, so that all missions in this area were built of perishable material, such as wooden logs, reeds, and a soft clay concrete. Stone was brought into eastern Texas for building forts and homes three quarters of a century later.)

On October 5, 1716, the mission was re-established, about six miles farther inland from the original site. The newly established mission was christened Nuestra Padre San Francisco de los Tejas. Father Manuel Castellanos was placed in charge of the settlement. Because of constant incitement of the nearby French, the Indians did not respond to the labors of the padres. In October, 1718, Governor Martin de Alarcon visited the mission and tried without success to persuade the Indians to join with the padres in forming a pueblo in the mission. Baptisms at the time totaled twenty.

In 1719 the French attacked Presidio los Adaes and a sister mission in the area. When news of this reached the priests of Nuestra Padre San Francisco de los Tejas, the mission was abandoned.

During the next three years there was no mission activity in eastern Texas. On August 5, 1721, after the French had withdrawn into Louisiana, the mission was re-established and rechristened San Francisco de los Neches. Very little is known of the history of this mission's activity other than an account given by General Pedro de Rivera, who visited the province in 1724. According to General Rivera's report, there was not an Indian at San Francisco de los Neches and there appeared little hope of any returning. The missionaries petitioned the viceroy for permission to move to an area where their labors would be more effective. The petition received viceregal sanction in October, 1729.

In early June, 1730, Mission San Francisco de los Neches was re-established on the banks of the Colorado River near present Austin, in the vicinity of Zilker Park. It was believed by Father

Miguel Sevillano, who was in charge of the mission, that the Colorado River would furnish water for the irrigation of the fields, but for some reason not recorded, Father Sevillano, on June 27, 1730, petitioned the viceroy for permission to move the mission to the San Antonio River, and on March 5, 1731, the mission was established at its final site near San Antonio and was renamed San Francisco de la Espada. (See Mission San Francisco de la Espada, under Missions Standing, pages 85–88)

NUESTRA SEÑORA DE LA GUADALUPE DE LOS NACOGDOCHES

Mission Nuestra Señora de la Guadalupe de los Nacogdoches was located on a site near the present city of Nacogdoches (Nacogdoches means persimmon eater), on a plain surrounded by shady trees, with a permanent creek that flowed through the grounds. It was founded by the Domingo Ramon expedition on July 9, 1716, and Father Antonio Margil de Jesus of the College of Zacatecas was placed in charge of the settlement.

The mission was surrounded by several Indian villages and the natives were quite friendly with the missionaries. For the first half century Mission Nuestra Señora de la Guadalupe de los Nacogdoches prospered, then it began to decline. A report made about 1765 states that there were no Indians residing at the mission and there was a look of forlornness about the place. The adobe church was still neat and orderly and had all things required for those who prayed and hoped, but the granary and the monastery for the padres and houses for the soldiers stationed there were rundown. The stockade surrounding the mission was missing poles, and its fields and orchards were poorly cultivated and tended. The Indians preferred to remain in their own villages rather than live in the mission and work. The orchard produced fine peaches and persimmons but they were left to rot on the trees. The Indians came to the mission on feast days and when gifts were to be had, or when sickness or fear of death drove them there. The old priest who was in charge of the mission at the time explained the deterioration of Nuestra Señora de la Guadalupe de los Nacogdoches as being the result of the massacre of San Saba and the failure of the Spanish to provide proper protection for the missions.

In 1719 the mission was abandoned when the French invaded Texas territory. Seven years later, on August 18, 1726, the Marquis de Aguayo restored Nuestra Señora de la Guadelupe de los Nacogdoches at a site on which present-day Nacogdoches is built. Three hundred and ninety Indians were present at the dedication. Father Antonio Margil de Jesus said High Mass, and the entire battalion of San Miguel de Aragon, organized into eight companies, was formed in front of the church and fired repeated salutes. The Indians were deeply impressed. Father Joseph Rodriguez was placed in charge as resident missionary. The saintly Father Margil took Rodriguez by the hand and led him in and out of the church and, doing likewise with the Indian chief who had been elected governor of the neophytes, he bestowed upon the mission sufficient lands and water for the sowing of crops and the raising of cattle. To conclude the occasion, the Marquis ordered that a great banquet be served to the missionaries, officers, and chiefs of the Indians.

In 1773, after Louisiana was ceded to Spain by the French, Nuestra Señora de la Guadalupe de los Nacogdoches was permanently abandoned. Its deserted buildings formed the nucleus for the settlement of the town of Nacogdoches by Gil Antonio Ibarov, in 1779.

NUESTRA SEÑORA DE LOS DOLORES DE LOS AIS

Mission Nuestra Señora de los Dolores de los Ais was first located about a mile south of present San Augustine. It was founded in February, 1717, by the Domingo Ramon expedition among the Ais Indians of east Texas. It became the headquarters for the Franciscan fathers of the College of Zacatecas in east Texas.

In 1719 the mission was abandoned because of the French invasions. In 1721, when the Marquis de Aguayo came to eastern Texas to re-establish the missions after the French left the area, he relocated Mission Nuestra Señora de los Dolores de los Ais. The former mission had been destroyed without a trace remaining. A location for the new mission was chosen, which was described as being "beside a stream, near a beautiful spring, on a high slope of ground from which a plain well suited for planting extended all around." The city of San Augustine claims that site today. The old mission stood on a conical slope, about half a mile south of the city, on the old King's Highway, at the edge of the bayou.

On August 23, 1721, when the mission was partly finished, High Mass was celebrated with all solemnity and the church was dedicated. About a hundred and eighty Indians had gathered for the occasion. After formalities were observed, the natives were urged to congregate in the stockade, at which time they elected an Indian chief to be governor of the neophytes, and the Maquis presented him with a new suit of fine cloth and a cane with silver mounting as the insignia of his office. Clothes and gifts were then distributed to all the Indians present.

Mission Nuestra Señora de los Dolores de los Ais was never the success expected of it. The Indians remained lazy and indifferent, showing enthusiasm only when gifts and other handouts were passed among them. Stealing became habitual at the mission, for now the Indians could trade the stolen articles to the nearby French for paint, bullets, and rum. Also, the soldiers took increasing liberties with the Indian maidens, for these Indian women were, according to the chronicle of a visiting priest, "very beautiful, tall and shapely, and they all had white, glittering teeth and nubile bodies."

In the summer of 1773 Nuestra Señora de los Dolores de los Ais was abandoned, but the Indians wishing to remain with the missionaries were transferred to San Antonio de Bexar. When the mission deteriorated, stone taken from its ruins went into many of the original buildings of San Augustine.

SAN ANTONIO DE VALERO

Mission San Antonio de Valero was located on the San Antonio River, at a site which is today in downtown San Antonio. Although permission for its founding was granted in 1716, the mission was not established until two years later on May 1, 1718. It was founded by Father Antonio de San Buenaventura Olivares under authority of the College of Queretaro. When first founded it had been called San Antonio de Padua.

Father Olivares had accompanied Father Isidro Felix de Espinosa on an expedition into Texas in 1709, at which time he studied the Indians, the locality, and the potentialities for irrigation water near the location of today's San Antonio. He reported his findings to the viceroy, who was sufficiently impressed to give his permission for the establishment of the mission. Two years passed before

Father Olivares returned to Texas. At Mission San Francisco de Solano, near Presidio San Juan Bautista on the lower Rio Grande, Father Olivares tarried to gather Indians who would act as interpreters and helpers in the establishment of the new mission. These Indians belonged to a tribe of Xarame and spoke a language similar to that of the tribes near the proposed site of the new mission. Church supplies, tools, seeds for planting, sheep, goats, and other necessities were taken along.

Father Olivares left the Rio Grande on April 18, 1718, nine days after the newly appointed general of the province, Martin de Alarcon, set out from Coahuila. On May 1, 1718, Father Olivares arrived at the San Antonio River where he united his Indians, herds, and baggage with the forces of General Alarcon. On that day Mission San Antonio de Valero was founded. It was called San Antonio in honor of Saint Anthony, and de Valero was added to its name to honor the viceroy who had made possible not only the founding of the mission but the establishment of a presidio and the founding of Villa de Bexar, which with the human enterprise, sweat, tears, toil, and common dogged perseverence of mankind in the end survived to become the present city of San Antonio. Father Olivares' judgment of the area was justified. Mission San Antonio de Valero prospered; and some of Texas' first and most successful missions were established there. San Antonio became the stronghold of Spanish occupation for the entire country.

Within two years Father Olivares' settlement was flourishing. Irrigation ditches had been opened, fields were planted, and large herds of sheep, goats, and horses and mares were abundant. In 1726, Mission San Antonio de Valero received the neophytes from Mission San Francisco Xavier de Naxera when that settlement was abandoned. San Antonio de Valero continued to prosper for many years, receiving neophytes from several other missions. It also had its depressions, but in the long run the recommendations of the astute Father Oliveras were brilliantly borne out, as the history of all the San Antonio missions proved. Royal orders for its secularization were issued in 1792 but were not carried out until 1793. Mission San Antonio de Valero passed through several periods and stages and uses, finally becoming the Alamo. (See Mission San Francisco Xavier de Naxera, under Missions Lost, page 71; and Mission San Antonio de Padua, under Missions Lost, page 70; and the Alamo, under Missions Ruins, page 140.)

MISSION DE LAS CABRAS

Mission de las Cabras was located four miles southeast of Floresville, on the San Antonio River. It was established in the mid 1720's at the insistence of Father Antonio de Jesus Marquez for the benefit of the Indians who were assigned to work on the Mission San Jose y Miguel de Aguayo ranch, which was approximately thirty miles from San Antonio.

Father Marquez ordered a chapel to be built on the ranch and a missionary was assigned to live there so that the Indians might receive Christian instruction without traveling to and fro between the ranch and San Jose. Accordingly, a church and monastery were constructed of stone and clay and a padre and two soldiers assigned in residence. For a dozen years Las Cabras served as a successful sub-mission of the settlement of San Jose y Miguel de Aguayo.

When established, the mission was called Los Cabreros (the goatherders). The ranch ran several thousand head of goats as well as other stock. Las Cabras served its purpose well, perhaps too well; for it lay directly on the route traveled by the Canary Islanders on their journey to San Antonio. As time passed and traffic increased, the mission was expanded. Full-scale mission plans were brought from San Antonio and work was begun on the chapel and monastery with the idea of developing it into an independent mission. When completed it had ample quarters for the Indian ranch workers, schoolrooms, workshops, its own granary, blacksmith shop and foundry; also it had adequate quarters for the transient families traveling from the coast to the settlement of San Antonio de Bexar. The stone and mortar wall around the mission had twenty loopholes for musket fire and was mounted with four cannon. Two missionaries and four soldiers were assigned regularly to the mission.

By 1778 Mission de las Cabras had lost its importance as a way station, and, as an independent mission, it fell into poverty, with only twenty-six inhabitants. When the soldiers were withdrawn it ceased to function. The old buildings were still standing and the wall was intact until the 1930's when the WPA used much of its stones for government projects. Thanks to the recent renaissance in Texas mission restoration, the old Mission de las Cabras will be preserved and spared from further deterioration.

The restored Mission Espiritu Santo de Zuniga.

ESPIRITU SANTO DE ZUNIGA

Mission Espiritu Santo de Zuniga, commonly called Espiritu Santo (or La Bahia Mission) was first located on Garcitas Creek at Matagorda Bay on the site of old Fort Saint Louis. It was founded April 6, 1722, by the Marquis de Aguayo and Father Agustin Patron, in an attempt to Christianize those Indians with whom the French had failed. The mission was established in conjunction with the presidio of Nuestra Señora de Loreto, which the Spaniards built on the ruins of La Salle's old Fort Saint Louis. The name of the presidio and mission eventually took its name from Matagorda Bay (La Bahia Espiritu Santo) and honored Baltasar de Zuniga by adding his name. Therefore it was formerly known as La Bahia del Espiritu Santo de Zuniga.

In 1726 the mission and presidio were moved to a site on the Guadalupe River, near present Victoria. That part of the country southeast of Victoria, in Victoria County, is still known as Mission Valley. In 1749, at the request of the missionaries, the mission and presidio were again moved and located on the banks of the San Antonio River at its final site, at present-day Goliad. Since the restoration of the mission chapel and the old presidio bastion, Mission Espiritu Santo de Zuniga has become known simply as Bahia Mission.

The fathers of the College of Zacatecas, under which authority Espiritu Santo was founded, greatly favored the location and planned with optimism and enthusiasm to develop, under the powerful protection of Presidio Bahia, a civil settlement such as existed at San Antonio de Bexar. As a result, a second mission was founded in 1754 about four miles west of the presidio. It was called Nuestra Señora del Rosario. While both missions prospered for a time, the plans for a settlement to rival San Antonio failed principally because the padres were not able to develop a system of irrigation at that location on the San Antonio River, and the missions had to rely on dry farming, which was inadequate. The river bed was too low and there were no natural springs here to supply the river as at San Antonio. As a result the San Antonio missions regularly sent huge supplies of vegetable and fruit and corn to sustain the La Bahia settlement.

At its height Espiritu Santo de Zuniga was in very good condition. The church was well provided with vestments, sacred vessels, and articles needed in the work of guiding souls. A lamp was kept burning at the door to assure the Indians of welcome at all times. To the right of the chapel, at a little distance, was the missionaries' quarters, offices and rooms for industry, such as weaving, pottery making and other mission industry. Directly behind these quarters can be traced the adobe and masonry upon which the original walls rose. To the left of the chapel and extending some distance ran another portion of the wall. Near one of the entrances was the blacksmith shop. All buildings were neat and comfortable, and the whole mission was surrounded by a substantial stockade. It was across the river from the presidio. There was no bridge over the stream and all communication was by means of a canoe.

Because of frequent shortage of rainfall, little or no corn was raised. When the weather was favorable cotton, melons, potatoes, and beans were raised. The mission owned an orchard where figs, apples, pears and peaches were grown successfully. Nonetheless, this mission, like Mission Nuestra Señora del Rosario and Presidio La Bahia, was never self-supporting.

Notwithstanding the strong protective arm of La Bahia, Mission Espiritu Santo de Zuniga was subjected to frequent raids and molestations by the Apaches who, ever fearful of their mortal enemies the Comanches, had begun to roam regularly to the south of San Antonio, becoming increasingly bold. Bands of Apaches repeatedly entered the mission, insulted the missionaries, and stole possessions —of the neophytes. This flaunting of the padres' authority had a tendency to demoralize the mission Indians, make them lose respect for the missionaries and disregard the benefits of mission life. In plain view of the mission the raiders slaughtered cattle and stole horses. Whenever the soldiers from the presidio gave chase, they were satisfied to retrieve the cattle and stock, and usually let the Indians go. This leniency only encouraged the marauders and increased the trouble for the missions.

In spite of Apache hostilities and uncertainty of the harvest and the many hardships suffered by the missionaries, the two La Bahia missions enjoyed a fair degree of prosperity. Espiritu Santo de Zuniga remained in operation until its was secularized in 1794. In 1818 it was converted into a school for the families of the soldiers and settlers. It later fell into the hands of the Presbyterian Church and was remade into a small denominational school called Aranama College. When the Civil War began, the entire student body left to enlist in the Confederate army. Shortly afterward it was reduced to ashes by fire. Restored, it is now part of Goliad State Park. (See Mission Nuestra Señora del Rosario, following; and Presidio La Bahia, page 128.)

NUESTRA SEÑORA DEL ROSARIO

Mission Nuestra Señora del Rosario (Our Lady of the Rosary) was located at present Goliad, about four miles west of Presidio La Bahia, where Mission Espiritu Santo de Zuniga and the old presidio have been gloriously restored. The Texas Highway Department has erected a monument on the site giving a history of the mission. Mission Rosario was founded in November, 1754, by missionaries of the College of Zacatecas, and was placed under the care of Father Juan Dios Maria Camberos.

With the strongly fortified bastion of Presidio La Bahia as a nucleus, and ideally located as it was on the San Antonio River between the settlement of San Antonio de Bexar and the coast, the missionaries of the College of Zacatecas were desirous of founding here a community rivaling that of San Antonio. Already Mission Espiritu Santo de Zuniga, just across the river from the presidio, showed great promise. So a second mission, Nuestra Señora del Rosario, was founded a little to the west, which would recruit its neophytes from the tribes of the coastal Karankawas Indians. To civilize and Christianize these seven-foot-tall cannibalistic Indians would indeed be an admirable accomplishment, so reasoned the undefeatable Franciscan friars.

Mission Señora del Rosario was larger and roomier than Espiritu Santo de Zuniga, averaging 300 feet in dimension. The buildings first erected were of wood covered with mud and plastered over with lime. Later, when the Indians had become subdued, they helped the missionaries build a new church in the mission, replacing the wooden one with an elaborate edifice of stone and concrete made of river-bed rock, gravel, and clay. They built a granary, quarters for the missionaries, and their own huts, which were of adobe and rock, with clay filling.

By the summer of 1758 Mission Nuestra Señora del Rosario had reached a flourishing state, although the Indians were still backward and continually gave trouble. Few had been baptized. There were four hundred neophytes, but Father Camberos had baptized only twenty-three. The mission had seven hundred head of cattle, one hundred and fifty sheep, and fifty horses. It had an old bell loaned to it by Epiritu Santo de Zuniga, an image of Nuestra Maria Santisima del Rosario, an old damask ornament given by the College of Zacatecas, a chalice, a paten, and all other articles necessary for divine worship. It had orchards of peaches, apples, and figs; fields of beans, potatoes, and sugar cane. But crops depended on the weather, which was not always favorable. Irrigation had not been successful in this location. For this reason the missionaries' dream of a settlement rivaling that of San Antonio failed.

Mission Nuestra Señora del Rosario was not without its troubles. The Indians were ever intractable; they were subject to all sorts of minor ills and diseases. Measles broke out frequently and there was grumbling that their idol gods were angry with them because they preferred the God of the missionaries. Medicine men added their evil work: they constantly hovered around the fields, agitating the neophytes to forsake the mission and return to their former way of life. Indians ran away and soldiers were sent to bring them back. Cattle and stock were frequently stolen.

One day a group of Indians deserted the mission, and the same day a soldier from the presidio disappeared. A half dozen soldiers were sent out to locate the Indians. After some time the soldiers met the escaped neophytes who were voluntarily returning to the mission. When questioned about the missing soldier, all were silent —and smug. At the mission, in possession of the wayward neophytes, buttons from the missing soldier's uniform were found. A rumor arose among the Indians that the delinquent group had taken a pleasant holiday and "had had a good feast."

By 1781 Mission Nuestra Señora del Rosario was in decline. Droughts had reduced the food supply and the Indians were forced to return to the chase; many went back to the coast and took up their old way of life. There were desertions because of Apache and Comanche raids. Livestock was stolen or needlessly killed. By the end of the century there were so few Indians at the mission that it was abandoned.

Today Mission Nuestra Señora del Rosario is just a trace of crumbled walls and mounds of fallen stones, including the base of the mission's church belfry tower. These are located near the park where Mission Espiritu Santo de Zuniga and Presidio La Bahia have been magnificently restored. (See Mission Espiritu Santo de Zuniga, preceding; and Presidio La Bahia, following.)

PRESIDIO LA BAHIA

Presidio La Bahia, although not a mission, deserves mention here because the story of its existence and function is inseparable from the history of Mission Espiritu Santo de Zuniga and Mission Nuestra Señora del Rosario. With the savage Apaches and Comanches to the west and north of them and the fierce Karankawas on their south, these two missions could not possibly have existed without the presence of the powerful bastion Presidio La Bahia. Moreover, a few highlights of this presidio will serve to illuminate the relationship between the presidios and missions that existed in Texas in the heyday of Spanish occupation.

Chapel of Presidio La Bahia, Goliad, Texas.

Presidio La Bahia and Mission Espiritu Santo de Zuniga had first been located on the site where La Salle's settlement had once stood. Ill treatment of the Indians by the Spanish officers and soldiers was the underlying cause of their removal. Officer discipline and soldier morale at the fort La Bahia had deteriorated and consequently Indian depredations increased. Cruelty, drunkeness and gambling were rampant among the soldiers, and there was little or no discipline. Logs of the stockade had been pulled away and used for firewood, and the defenses were in a careless condition. But the soldiers were supremely happy, mainly because they could, at will, take full liberties with the maiden Indian neophytes. As a consequence of this poor discipline and bad conduct of the soldiers the Indians raided the fort frequently, killed soldiers, and stole the stock.

One day while an Indian was waiting for his cut of beef from a freshly killed cow at the mission, he decided to shake out his blanket. Unfortunately, the dust fell in a cloud upon the corn being

Ancient entrance of the La Bahia structure.

The crumbling walls outside La Bahia.

ground by the wife of one of the officers of the presidio. The woman, enraged, summoned her husband to give the hapless Indian a punishment of lashes. The Indian resisted and a fight between him and the officer occurred, in which the officer received a knife wound. The Indian was seized and was about to be put to death, when the rest of the natives became aroused and about forty took up their bows and arrows and attacked the soldiers, wounding many; they then fled to the woods with their families and belongings.

Captain Jose Domingo Ramon, commanding officer at the presidio, was at a ranch a few miles away at the time of the disturbance. Word was sent to him. Accompanied by a mount of soldiers he went in pursuit of the runaway Indians. He overtook them after a short distance, and by promising them absolution from punishment if they would return to the mission, persuaded them to lay down their bows and arrows and accompany him back to the presidio.

Once inside the presidio, Captain Ramon ordered them confined to a hut, and from this overcrowded prison they were to be summoned one by one for remonstration, at which time he promised to give each a portion of beef from a freshly killed animal slaughtered before their eyes in the yard. This was a sadistically cruel trick. The Indians could plainly see the soldiers preparing the hanging ropes, and they refused to budge from their confine. Captain Ramon, with an air of supreme confidence, entered the hut and tried to persuade them of his friendship and to entice them outside to partake of the meat. When he thought he had succeeded, he shouted to his soldiers: "At them! Kill them!"

The Indians tried to break away, and one of them managed to stab Captain Ramon in the chest with the blade of a pair of scissors. The soldiers fired their muskets into the hut and trained a cannon upon it. A few of the Indians got away, but a young maiden was the only one they were able to catch. Captain Ramon ordered that she be hanged in view of the soldiers. Eight days later he died of the wound he had received.

When Presidio La Bahia and Mission Espiritu Santo de Zuniga were removed to their present location, the presidio got a new lease on life. It was garrisoned with efficient officers and fresh soldiers. Morale became excellent. Everyone was pleased with the new site on the San Antonio River at Goliad. (The town received its name from a legendary Indian called Goliath, an "unbeliever, great in bulk and stature." It was at Goliad that Colonel James Fannin, after the Alamo massacre, surrendered to General Santa Anna "with terms of honor," and whereupon Santa Anna ordered the shooting of his entire force of approximately four hundred men, including Colonel Fannin. Thus rose the battle cry at San Jacinto: "Remember the Alamo; remember Goliad!") The new bastion was built atop a rugged hill, a location with tactical advantage against assault combined with a nearby supply of water. When completed, Presidio La Bahia covered a rectangular area 370 feet long by 350 feet wide, and was stoutly built of large wooden beams and river-bed rock and lime mortar. The armament of the presidio consisted of six eight-pounders brought in by water from Vera Cruz, Mexico. Of these, four were mounted on gun carriages, while the other four were mounted at the wall bastions. There were also two swivel guns properly mounted.

The garrison consisted of eighty men, and it was kept up to full strength, all vacancies being promptly filled. Three soldiers were assigned to Mission Espiritu Santo de Zuniga and four more to the newly established Mission Nuestra Señora del Rosario because it was farther away and more exposed to Indian attacks. The soldiers not only protected the padres and mission Indians and their property, inspiring proper respect, but helped them to instruct the neophytes in their daily tasks. In the presidio ten men were kept constantly on day and night guard duty. Seven more were used to escort supply trains required to bring corn, vegetables, and other goods from San Antonio, since the two missions did not raise sufficient food to sustain themselves or the presidio.

In spite of its excellent morale and high efficiency the presidio could not escape its share of mischief from recalcitrant Indians. There was the case of the Indian overseer who called himself Jose Maria. He had a keen mind and was exceptionally enterprising. He learned quickly, acquired a fluent command of Spanish, and became the pride of the mission friars; he also commanded great respect from the Indians of the entire area.

The mission fathers had great confidence in Jose Maria and entrusted him with arms and duties away from the settlement. In 1778 he was sent with an accompaniment of Indians to the coast, a day's journey, to bring back some supplies that had arrived by boat. Louis Landrin, the captain of the ship, received Jose Maria and his Indian band hospitably with food and drink. Suddenly, at a signal from Jose, all the Indians drew pistols and murdered Landrin and his entire crew.

Jose Maria and his savages roamed the plains area between the coast and Presidio La Bahia for weeks and were finally caught. Jose was hanged for his crime.

Because his own people looked upon him as a hero, Jose Maria's death touched off a series of crime waves and depredations against the missions and murders of many settlers; Indians deserted the missions wholesale all along the San Antonio River.

Jose Maria's boldness incited another Indian to crime. He was Manuel Alegre, a resident of Nuestra Señora del Rosario mission. Soldiers from Presidio La Bahia had to be called in to quell the riots incited by Alegre.

A Karankawa chief, Frezada Pinta (Painted Blanket), always influenced his people to oppose the Spanish, but was subtler than his fellow renegades. He pretended to be a Christian, presented a peaceful attitude, and always spoke of friendliness for the missionaries, especially whenever gifts were to be distributed among his people. Yet Painted Blanket was an insidious troublemaker, until finally found out and banished.

Eternal fighting and bickering worked against the La Bahia missions. Indians deserted and returned to their savage way of life. Thousands of head of cattle were stolen and slaughtered or driven off by the Indians. In 1794 the two missions under La Bahia's protection came under the general secularization order; Nuestra Señora del Rosario was abandoned in 1807, but Espiritu Santo de Zuniga continued to be used as a fort by the Mexican Republic until 1821.

In 1812 three hundred adventurers under the leadership of Bernardo Gutierrez and Augustus Magee, in an attempt to capture the Texas territory, stormed Presidio La Bahia and captured it. Two thousand Spanish troops marched from San Antonio and placed La Bahia under siege, which lasted four months. Magee committed suicide within the fort and Gutierrez asked to talk terms. The terms of surrender proved unacceptable and he rejoined his men inside the fort, took the offensive, and routed the Spanish troops, pursued them to San Antonio where he defeated and captured them and had their officers slain. Gutierrez's forces were finally defeated and routed by an army from Mexico. Eight hundred of his men were put to death.

In the fall of 1821 La Bahia was stormed and taken by Dr. James Long, another would-be conqueror of Texas. Dr. Long was taken prisoner, carted off to Mexico, where he was shot upon release from prison.

Presidio La Bahia was also used as a bastion by the Texas colonists in their fight for the independence of Texas. Restored, today it commands the heights overlooking the San Antonio River in all its early glory. (See Mission Espiritu Santo de Zuniga, page 124, and Mission Nuestra Señora del Rosario, preceding.)

Mission of San Saba (now undergoing restoration).

MISSION SAN SABA

Mission San Saba, located a mile north of present Menard, was established in April 1757 by Colonel Diego Ortiz Parilla and Father Alonzo Giraldo de Terreros. It was dangerously exposed to both Comanche and Apache attack but it felt secure because it was directly under the wing of fortified and well-garrisoned Presidio San Louis de los Amarillas (Presidio San Saba).

San Saba was founded for the purpose of civilizing and Christianizing the plains Indians, chiefly the Apaches and Comanches, the most "unfriendly" of the Texas territory natives. Ironically, the mission is remembered for its massacre and destruction by the Comanches (with the help of some other tribes besides the Apaches), because the Comanches wanted to break up the alliance between their two foremost enemies, the Apaches and the Spaniards.

Weeks and months passed and no Indians came to live in the new mission. But the ever hopeful Franciscan friars never gave up. There were three at San Saba: Father Alonzo Giraldo Terteros, Father Jose Santiesteban, and Father Miguel Molina. From time to time scattered bands of Indians would stop temporarily to rest in the mission and enjoy its liberal hospitality. But they consistently refused to stay. All the while reports reached the presidio that Indians were gathering in great number in the north to form an attack on the settlement and destroy it with one blow.

When the attack did not come that winter, the rumors ceased to alarm the soldiers at the presidio and life settled down to an even tenor. Of the several hundred persons living there, two hundred and thirty seven were women and children. In April, however, rumors of an impending attack grew more persistent. In March, Indians were frequently seen about the area, and horses were continually stolen. There seemed little doubt now that the northern tribes were gathering preparatory to an attack upon San Saba, which included eighteen persons in all: the three missionaries, five soldiers guarding the mission, and ten Tlascalteca Indians. The mission was armed with two cannons and a supply of ammunition and was surrounded by a well-built stockade. The garrison of the presidio was weakened by four soldiers who had been sent to guard a mission on the Guadalupe, by seven who were attending the cattle on a ranch twelve miles away, and the five at San Saba Mission. The women and children at the presidio, too, gave the commandant uneasy thoughts.

On March 16, 1759, Comanches, Tuacanes, Toavayases, Vidais and Gueissuis, numbering some two thousand and led by several Apache chiefs, poured down upon the mission. The savages were armed with guns, pikes, sabers, lances, and bows and arrows; they were in war paint and dressed in war costumes of skins. Father Alonzo had just finished saying mass when the yells and animal calls of the Indians rent the air. The padres barred the doors of

the stockade as the main body of the Indians rushed to the mission
firing in the air. At the gate the wily denizens of the plains resorted
to treachery to gain entrance. With many signs and broken Spanish
they pretended friendship. Ascendo Cadena, one of the Spanish
soldiers, peered through the crack of the stockade and recognized
among the gathered Indians a number from tribes with whom he
previously had had good relations. Misled by the presence of these
former friends of the Spaniards, he convinced Father Alonzo that
the Indians were on a friendly call and advised him to open the
barricade. The bloodthirsty savages poured into the mission with
anything but friendly motives and whatever hope the good friars
had of peace vanished. Father Santiesteban retired to the chapel and
knelt in prayer.

While some of the intruders shook hands with appropriate signs
of friendship, accepting the tobacco and other gifts the friars were
handing out, the main body shamelessly began to pillage the store-
rooms, the kitchen, offices, and other private quarters.

The invaders emptied the corral of horses and demanded to
know where there were more. Father Alonzo, thinking to divert
them, told them that there were more horses at the presidio. The
Indian chief, who wore the shambles of a gaudy French uniform,
suspected a trick. To pacify him Father Alonzo hurriedly wrote a
note to the captain of the presidio and told the chief that with
this token they would be welcomed.

In a few minutes the chief returned, his face glowing with
anger. He had been fired upon and two of his warriors had been
killed and a number wounded. It became clear now that the mission
could expect no help from the presidio. Father Alonzo tried to
appease him. He climbed on a horse and started out with Jose
Garcia, a soldier, to accompany the Indians to the presidio. They
had gone but a little way when a shot rang out, and Father Alonzo
Giraldo de Terreros, who had labored an adult lifetime for the
Apaches, fell from his horse mortally wounded. Volleys of shots
followed; Garcia was killed outright. From some quarter the signal
was given for the massacre to begin.

The Spaniards in the mission fought desperately to reach a
haven of safety. Two of them, Lazaro de Ayala and Enrique Gutierrez, were shot down immediately and their bodies cut to pieces.
Father Molina, with a broken arm, gathered eight survivors, most
of them wounded, and they managed to barricade themselves in a

residence house. An orgy of blood and fire followed. An Apache, wielding a saber, came upon Father Santiesteban who was praying at the altar of Saint Francis. With a single blow he decapitated the priest.

The Indians danced and shouted wildly as they set fire to the church and the buildings. With fiendish glee they disrobed the bodies of Father Santiesteban and Father Alonzo and desecrated their bodies. They tossed Father Santiesteban's head among them as if it were a ball. The images of the saints in the chapel were cut to pieces, the cattle in the corral were slaughtered, and everything that could not be carried away was wantonly destroyed. Meanwhile the flames enveloped the buildings where the survivors were barricaded. When the besieged could no longer bear the heat and flames, they made a break for safety. Only four made it to the presidio. After destroying all the livestock and laying waste the fields, the Indians finally departed to the north, not chancing an attack on the presidio.

Mission San Saba had proved a tragic failure and the savage massacre terminated missionary work at this location. But it did not lessen the stout-hearted Franciscan fathers' determination to labor in behalf of the ungrateful Apaches. They moved to other places and other duties. In recent times restoration work has been done at the original site of Mission San Saba.

NUESTRA SEÑORA DEL REFUGIO

Mission Nuestra Señora del Refugio was initially located at the juncture of the San Antonio and the Colorado rivers, on Goff Bayou in Calhoun County. A marker was placed at the site by the Texas Centennial Commission in 1936. The settlement was later moved to the present site of the city of Refugio, which took its name from the old mission. It was established in 1793 by Father Joseph Francisco Mariano Garza by authority of the College of Zacatecas.

Mission Refugio's first location was chosen in the hope of attracting the runaway Indians from the missions in the interior. Indians of the Karankawas tribes, those giant-sized cannibalistic Gulf Coast natives, were continually leaving the La Bahia missions of Nuestra Señora del Rosario and Esperitu Santo de Zuniga and going back to their original habitat. Mission Refugio got many of these refugees. But Refugio's unhealthful location soon drove them away. They suffered from fever and stomach ailments. So in 1794 Mission Refugio was moved away from the coast and located at the site of the present town of Refugio.

Nuestra Señora del Refugio was the last mission to be established in Texas, and it was the last to be secularized. It was exempt from the general secularization order of 1794 because the missionaries there asked for more time to complete the instructions of its neophytes. Refugio's record of baptisms was kept until 1828. After all the Indians had abandoned the mission, it was auctioned off.

There are interesting remains to be found at the old site, but the church proper has disappeared. The old mission was so badly damaged during the Texas revolution that the Irish settlers of the section tore down the scarred remnants and built a large modern church on the site.

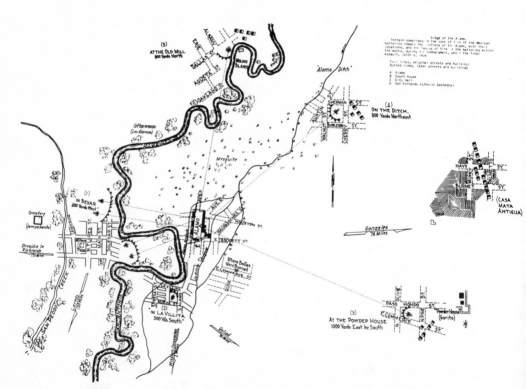

Plan of the Alamo fort along with a map of San Antonio.

The Alamo.

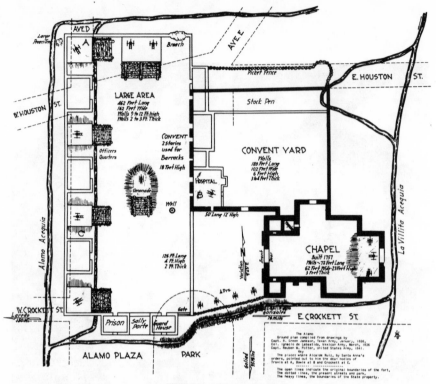

THE ALAMO

The old "mission" one may see today in midtown San Antonio at the Alamo Plaza is indeed a far cry from the original Mission San Antonio de Valero; or, for that matter, from the "Alamo Fort," in which one hundred and eighty-three American colonizers died in the final hours of March 6, 1836, in the fight for Texas independence. The casual visitor to the Alamo is likely to come away with a shockingly erroneous notion of what the early mission really was, or as it appeared. Little of the old mission and hardly any of the 1836 fort is preserved. What one sees is a rebuilt structure arranged to accommodate the real estate set aside for the Alamo shrine. Except for the entrance what remains of the original is architecturally unimportant. However, of all shrines in Texas, the Alamo (Mission San Antonio de Valero) is most endeared in the hearts of patriots, for it is considered the cradle of Texas liberty, hallowed in the history of Texas independence.

Before Mission San Antonio de Valero came to rest at its present location, in the heart of the modern city of San Antonio, it had other beginnings and another site, "two gun shots" distant from its present location. Before it was the Alamo or San Antonio de Valero it had other names. When first authorized, in 1716, it was called San Antonio de Padua. Father Antonio de San Buenaventura Olivares, who had some seven years earlier visited Texas and noted the "rich productiveness of the soil and the plentiful water supply" in the region of present San Antonio, had made cogent recommendations to the viceroy to establish a settlement in that area. So convincing were Father Olivares' arguments that the viceroy, Marquis de Valero, appointed Martin de Alarcon general-governor of the province and authorized the establishment of a presidio and Father Oliveras' mission. The presidio was to be called San Antonio de Bexar and the mission San Antonio de Padua.

Returning to Texas two years later by way of the Rio Grande, Father Oliveras gathered Indians from the Mission San Francisco Solano (formerly Mission San Ildefonso), which was on the Rio Grande River near present Presidio, and after collecting church equipment, tools for building and farming, seeds for planting, and other baggage, he proceeded northeast to the San Antonio River where he joined his forces with those of Alarcon, who had just arrived. They combined missions San Francisco Xavier de Naxera with Mission San Antonio de Padua, for which two years since Father Oliveras had secured authorization. On May 1, 1718, he christened the combined missions San Antonio de Valero, naming Saint Anthony as its patron, and adding de Valero to honor the viceroy who had made it possible.

The Saint Anthony to whom Mission San Antonio de Valero was dedicated was a Portugese by birth, saint of Padua, and ranks next to Saint Francis of Assisi as the most important saint. Teacher and preacher, Anthony of Padua was also a performer of miracles. Among the many to his credit, this one is recounted most frequently: At the funeral of a rich man he exclaimed, "His heart is buried upstairs in his treasure chest; go seek it there and you will find it." Whereupon the dead man's friends broke open the chest and, to their surprise, found the heart. Then they examined the body and found that, indeed, his heart was wanting.

In 1718, Mission San Antonio de Valero, as has been noted, was "two gun shots" distant from the location of the present Alamo shrine. It was originally a small mission, approximately 225 feet square, and was built of rock, adobe, wood, and clay mortar. It was destroyed after only a few years by a hurricane that swept inland from the Gulf of Mexico. Rebuilt on its present location (Alamo Plaza), its plans called for a more extensive and much larger mission. The walls were first thrown up, then the monastery, and after other necessary buildings, construction of the chapel was begun. Tradition has it that in building this mission mortar was mixed with asses' milk which the priests consecrated. This has given rise to some persons' belief that it was the only liquid used in mixing mortar for masonry in Texas missions. In the light of the number of asses this would necessitate and the torture in providing so much milk, the story becomes fabulous, as do many of the mission legends when put to the test of reality.

Spanish army engineers and the Franciscan fathers spared no expense or effort to make a formidable settlement of the new Mission San Antonio de Valero. The original fortifications which surrounded the mission and pueblo had little in common with the timid walls one sees today at Alamo Plaza. The original extended north across Houston Street enclosing some of the plot of the Federal Building, and south to Crockett Street; it reached east to beyond Nacogdoches Street, and swept westward across Alamo Plaza to the banks of the San Antonio River (which at that time ran parallel to the wall). This, then, was the largest of all Texas missions, with average dimension of over 400 feet. It was also one of the best fortified. All around the walls were loopholes for musket fire, and over the gate was a turret where three cannon were mounted. As a precaution against a siege, a good well had been dug behind the chapel to provide the inmates with an unlimited supply of water. Thus it may be seen that the mission was conditioned as a fort early in its existence.

The new San Antonio de Valero Mission was built of limestone taken from the quarries along the river. The church, however, begun in 1738, was poorly constructed; it was thrown up on dirt embankments and soon collapsed. With characteristic determination and industry the Franciscan friars began anew, building carefully with stone and well-congealed mortar; yet the church, although used for many years, was never completed. The chapel supported two towers flanking a carved doorway. The baptistry and chapel was located at the front, the nave proceeding five bays to a crossing where, past a transept projected out on either side, one entered the sanctuary. The plan was almost identical to that of the preserved Mission La Purisima Concepcion. An early description of the sacristy gives this picture: ". . . A well furnished room with drawers and closets in which the ornaments were kept. There were three chalices with their patens, four cruets, a mounted crucifix, a censer, and three anointers, all of silver. For the celebration of the Holy Sacrifice and other liturgical functions there were fourteen complete sets of vestments, some of Persian silk and some of damask, besides four copes. There were also twenty chalices and fifteen sets of altar cloths. The mission had three missals, two rituals, and all the things necessary for adequate celebration of the various festivals."

On the right hand side of the church (extending to the far side of what today is Houston Street) stretched the walled patio bordered by buildings with two-storied arched galleries. In these were offices and rooms for workshops and storage of materials. There was a large hall where there were four looms. Here cotton and woolen cloth and blankets of various kinds were woven to supply all the needs of the mission. Adjoining the looms were two rooms in which were kept the wool, the cotton, the combs, cards, spools, and other spinning accessories used by the Indians in the daily tasks. Both the wool and cotton used were raised by the mission. On the ground floor were the shops for heavier manufacture, such as iron works, the blacksmith shop, brick and tile making.

The quarters for the neophytes consisted of buildings arranged in a square of several tiers, through the center of which ran a waterway shaded by willows and some fruit trees. All houses were provided with doors and windows and each one had bunk-type beds and chests of drawers. Each family had its pots and pans and all necessary utensils, supplied from the common warehouse. In the granary, which was a large stone building, the supplies were kept. Here there was room for as many as eighteen hundred bushels of corn and several hundred bushels of beans, which were the annual harvest raised by the mission Indians. For the cultivation of their crops, chiefly corn, beans, chili, cotton, and some vegetables, the mission had forty yokes of oxen fully equipped, thirty plows and the necessary plowshares and harrows; twelve carts to transport supplies, stone and timber; fifty axes, forty hoes, twenty-two bars and twenty-five scythes. For carpentry they had all the necessary instruments and tools, such as planes, saws, vices, hammers, files, chisels, and braces. They also had a well-equipped blacksmith shop to repair their tools, sharpen their instruments, and shoe their stock.

Beyond the mission irrigation ditches had been constructed, fields were planted, and orchards flourished. The mission also had extensive ranch lands, which grazed large herds of cattle, horses, mares, mules, and goats and sheep. Mission San Antonio de Valero, at the height of its prosperity, was one of the most prosperous of the Spanish missions. It was during its abundant and happy years that its Indians were responsible for repelling an attack on the town of San Antonio de Bexar, saving its inhabitants from massacre.

The Apaches planned to take the town by attack, overthrow the presidio, destroy its inhabitants and burn the settlement. For some unknown reason, in this attack, the Apaches were not organized with their usual warlike efficiency when they advanced on the settlement. They split their forces, one contingent moving on the presidio and the others remaining in ambush just outside the town. An Indian boy, outside the mission looking for ripe melons in the field, spotted the Indians in ambush and ran into the mission to give the alarm. The padres quickly armed about one hundred neophytes with bows and arrows and guns and ammunition which was kept for such purposes. Led by an Apache convert, the hundred strong charged the invaders. The Apaches now separated into several bands and tried to advance into the city by different streets, but were thrown back at every point by the mission Indians.

Afterward the neophytes believed that success in defeating the invaders was owing to the Cross; and as if in confirmation of this belief, two months after the raid a squaw, bearing a cross and accompanied by a boy, came to San Antonio bringing gifts and a request for peace between the settlement and the Apaches.

Mission San Antonio de Valero maintained its level of prosperity and abundance for the next thirty years. Then it began to decline. By 1790 its disintegration was so complete that by orders of the Spanish viceroy the mission was secularized and its lands, its oxen, cows, tools, and seed were divided among the neophytes.

Thus, as is chronicled, the history of the Alamo encompasses the story of four Spanish missions: San Ildefonso, San Francisco Solano, San Francisco Xavier de Naxera and San Antonio de Valero (and a fifth in name only: San Antonio de Padua). In its later years it came to be known as the Alamo after a popular Spanish military organization, Compania Valante del Alamo, which was housed there in 1803. The word *alamo* means cottonweed, or poplar; these trees, great favorites among the early padres, once surrounded the old mission.

Of the Alamo chapel, which today stands amid busy downtown San Antonio, only the lower portion of the façade is original. The remainder of the church, as well as the walls surrounding the patio, are reconstructed. In 1849, when repair work was being done on the structure, the upper part of the façade was finished in its present shape. A new roof was added; and to assist in bearing up this roof, two stone pillars were built inside the transept. A second floor was added, and in the southwest tower, once a belfry, an office was made. The church serves as a museum commemorating the Battle of the Alamo and is in most part a modern structure raised on the foundations of the original. After its abandonment it served such purposes as a military quartermaster depot, a military hospital, and was at one time privately owned and used as a mercantile warehouse. Finally, the State of Texas purchased the property and the Daughters of the Republic of Texas assumed responsibility for its maintenance.

One must observe closely to appreciate the former glory of the old church. The architectural scheme of the original can be depicted only at the main entrance. It is remarkable that so delicate a piece of design ever escaped the ravages of gunfire, neglect, and the erosion of time. The motif is centered on a curved arched door six feet wide and twelve feet high, and capped with a keystone which, with the adjoining surface of the wall, is covered with a flat continuous carving. It is the richness of this ornamentation—endless twining arabesques and foliage forms making the stone shimmer with little shadows of light—that the Moorish detail is felt.

On either side of the doorway are coupled columns between which are niches that once sheltered stone images, one of San Francisco and one of Santo Domingo, but they have long since disappeared. The four columns, set just away from the wall, are three feet off the ground on paneled pedestals, the lower half being fluted while the upper half twists in spiral channels. This is expressive of the late Renaissance tempered by Mexican tastes. The window above this is a square in design and lacks decoration, as if a second artist took over and disapproved of the former's taste. The rest of the façade is the work of restoration.

Nowhere in the world is there a student of history who has not heard of the glory of the Alamo. The "Battle of the Alamo," the "Massacre of the Alamo," the "Stand at the Alamo" has been told and retold. It has been solemnized in hymnal and verse; it has been re-enacted and filmed at the cost of millions of dollars. It will be retold again and again—until the end of recorded time. It will not be amiss, then, to tell it once again. All writers of Alamo stories have been guilty of one common fault: they begin their stories with the premise that all those who died in the Alamo were heroes at the outset. In the account that follows it was taken into consideration that the hundred and eighty-three men who died there were first mere mortals, then heroes.

12

Death over the Alamo– The Bloody Birth of Texas Independence

I T is Sunday. The year is 1836, the day, March 6. The stage is set for one of the most terrible and glorious Sundays in the history of Texas. The bloody drama is to be enacted within the two-and-a-half-acre area of the former San Antonio de Valero mission, called the Alamo. As the curtain rises the earth, spinning in implacable habitude, has wheeled off a hundred and twelve minutes of this memorable Sunday.

1:52 A.M.

A man, naked to the waist, lies in his marquee scarcely four hundred yards from the dark, brooding Alamo, dozing the euphoric half sleep, half dream of one well-dosed with morphine. His head rests on the bare legs of a girl hardly fourteen. She languidly fans away the big slow-flying mosquitoes from the man's handsome face; occasionally she bends over him to snatch at one of the hungry parasites about to light on his bare chest, and in so doing her naked, firm breasts brush his cheek. Soon the man will awake from his self-induced sleep. Soon the final assault will begin. The man is General Antonio Lopez de Santa Anna Perez de Lebron, president of the Republic of Mexico. He is on this night forty-two years and thirteen days old. This child-mistress is not the first in his life. She is only one in a long list of nymphets that this remarkable and terrible man is to acquire in his eighty-two years of exciting and stormy life.

147

2:02 A.M.

Lieutenant Colonel William Barrett Travis crouches atop the three-foot-wide stone and adobe wall surrounding the mission. The near-full moon, intermittently obscured by scuds of cold and white clouds, lights the chalky plain around the Alamo. A chill north wind is blowing over the sixteen-foot wall. Colonel Travis hopes it will not stir up his "lung fever" and bring on a spasm of coughing. This would alert the enemy and put an end to his reconnaissance.

The slow-moving river, fed by early spring rains, has crept over its confines and lies like the wide shimmering blade of a huge bolo knife around the southeastern perimeter of the mission wall. Santa Anna, the Mexican general, has had the area between the river and the mission cleared of brush trees, live oaks, cacti and mesquite; when the charge comes there is to be no impedimenta. Out there, Colonel Travis estimates, are four thousand Mexican soldiers. Inside the walls of the Alamo are one hundred and eighty-three Americans. In the farthermost bend of the river and a good three hundred yards distant, he can see the Mexican army headquarters. General Santa Anna's marquee glows red from the busy lights inside, and stirring figures reflect their dark shadows on the translucent fabric. Outside and around the headquarters, too, there is feverish activity.

Two flags are pulsating in the night breeze above Santa Anna's marquee. One is the new Republic of Mexico flag, designed by President-General Santa Anna himself for the nation he has recently taken over by force. It embodies the despot's cynical hypocrisy, the big lie without which no dictator can succeed in his megalomaniacal mission. There is a tricolor of white, green, and red in vertical stripes—white denoting the purity of the Catholic Church, green for independence, red for the union of the Spanish element with the Mexican; and in one corner the national coat of arms: an eagle perched on a cactus holding a snake in his beak— the famous Eagle and Serpent of Aztec mythology.

The other flag, truly representative of Santa Anna, the man himself, is the blood-red "no quarter" flag, which the Mexican general had ordered raised ten days ago when Colonel Travis answered with a cannon shot his "surrender at discretion" demand. The blood red flag means that the assault upon the Alamo will be inspired by the *degüello,* whose not-unpleasant notes are associated with "no quarter." It has for centuries been the signal for beheading and throat-cutting. Spain had used the call in her long war with the Moors and it had meant the wanton destruction of both lives and property. It is the fire and death call, exhorting soldiers to extreme mercilessness. Ironically, another blood-red flag flies from the dome of San Fernando Cathedral in the heart of the old town, placed there by Santa Anna himself for all to see. Santa Anna has vowed to exterminate the Texas force, to make an example of them and to frighten the Americans into submission and so open the way for Mexican domination to the Pacific coast.

Colonel Travis raises himself cautiously. For long minutes he watches and listens. In the darkness he can hear the shuffling of thousands of feet, sandals clopping on the chalky ground as the various battalions form into columns of attack. About a hundred yards out, arrayed in a semicircle, is the Mexican artillery, consisting mainly of two- and four-pounders with several heavier pieces and the two howitzers, which he judges to be twelve-pounders.

According to the commitment of their heavy weaponry, the main assault will be concentrated upon the northeast wall. This section of the wall is the weakest; it is lower and therefore below the range of the cannon mounted atop the chapel located at the opposite section of the compound. It was here that, four days ago, the Mexicans placed a huge charge of powder and blew away a section. Colonel James Bowie and his men, however, had quickly closed the breach and thrown up a lunette of earthen breastworks and mounted two four-pounders. Inside the circle of Mexican cannon and about fifty yards from the wall, Santa Anna's cavalry is being drawn up. In front of the cavalry and almost directly under the wall, *los zapadores,* Santa Anna's engineers, together with the infantry, are forming. In the semidarkness Travis enumerates eighteen scaling ladders, eleven axes, and three huge iron crowbars being brought up.

Santa Anna's strategy brings into focus the savagery that lurks in the brain of this self-styled "Napoleon of the West." His own soldiers have orders to cut down any of their comrades who falter or retreat. If the *zapadores* are repulsed his cavalry will turn them back or cut them to pieces. Should the cavalry, somehow thwarted, become disorganized by fire from the bastion and fail in this grisly duty, the artillery will turn its cannon on the combined units. It is to be a do-or-die attack.

There is little doubt in Colonel Travis's mind about the outcome of this battle. The hundred and eighty-three Americans inside the mission—many sick, all fatigued and hungry, their water supply cut off—cannot by sane man's reasoning long withstand Santa Anna's cannon, gun, bayonet, and sword. For days Travis and his staff have known that no relief can be expected from General Sam Houston in Austin or Colonel James Fannin at Goliad. In fact, General Houston had ordered Colonel Travis, in command of the regulars and the cavalry, and Colonel Bowie, in command of the Volunteer Aid, to abandon the Alamo, blow up its works, fall back and join Fannin's forces at Goliad and march the combined forces on Austin to reinforce the main Texas army. Led by Bowie, the little force behind the walls of the Alamo bastion has held a consultation and elected to remain in the Alamo and fight, in direct contradiction to Houston's orders. "Victory or death!" had become their cry.

Colonel Travis is about to lower himself from the wall when he hears the grating of a ladder against the masonry. Mexican scouts on the wall! He creeps silently forward, his hand closing around the polished black walnut grip of his Golcher single-shot pistol. Excitement flushes his feverish cheeks. Since coming to Texas, this frenzied twenty-seven-year-old lawyer-soldier has learned to relish the taste for killing. He will never leave Texas. Here he has found killing a commonplace thing—a not unpleasant commonplace. It has become a kind of drug that demands larger and larger doses. The supreme feeling, bright, exhilarating, which killing gives him has become a solace, a kind of insane balm for his troubled soul. He kills and then he can forget Rosana for a little while. The excitement of killing kindles a quick fire in his searing, dying lungs, and they betray him. He coughs. Instantly flattening himself on the wall—he listens.

Silently his boot finds footing in the masonry, and with the relaxed alertness of a cat he waits. The Mexican, incautious, unwisely leaps in the direction of human sound. Travis fires. The Mexican, in midair, does not feel the ball of the smooth-bore Golcher as it passes clean through his breast from left lung to right shoulder. He experiences only a sudden vast emptying of strength as the blood spurts, as if from a fountain, directly from his heart onto the prostrate Travis. He gives a groan, not out of pain but rather of surprise: how quick and quiet and painless death can be.

"*Dios! Dios! Dios!* . . ."

Travis pushes the Mexican's body from the wall, wipes the man's blood off his tunic, lets himself down into the courtyard. That will put an end to the enemy reconnaissance. What intelligence did Santa Anna seek? The three traitors who went over to the Mexicans last night surely told all there is to know. Now he must call the men together. But first to see Bowie.

Bowie! Jim Bowie, the fighting man! What a loss, Travis reflects. Fate had dealt Bowie a double blow. First a typhoid-pneumonia had laid him low; then, the very first day Surgeon Amos Pollard had allowed him off his cot, weakened and not fully recovered, he had dislocated a hip in a fall from a scaffolding while helping the men position one of the heavy cannon on the roof of the chapel. Unable to stand on his feet after the accident, he had turned over command of his volunteers to Travis, thirteen years his junior.

2:41 A.M.

As Colonel Travis crosses the yard he glances at the sky. As if numbers were not enough, the weather, too, is with the Mexicans. The wind has cleared away the clouds. There will be no morning fog to foul the Mexican guns. The Mexican armament, he reflects, consists of flint firelock pieces requiring the use of exposed powder. Rain or heavy fog would foul them and they would misfire. The infantry is equipped with *escopetas,* short carbine-type rifles, with flintlock plates, and .69-caliber flint muskets and a few old-fashioned *miquelets,* whose mainspring is on the outside of the lock plate and exposed. They are especially short on pistols, with only a scattering of muzzle-loaders and these mainly in the hands of officers. The *escopetas* and pistols are short-range weapons and inaccurate; once fired, they require a lapse of time for reloading. At close quarters the Mexicans are prone to abandon them in preference to bayonets and sabers, with which they are far more proficient. The Americans have flintlocks, too, but many of them are in possession of converted cap-and-ball rifles and percussion pistols, which they have brought with them from the East. The Americans are deadly marksmen—all.

William Barrett Travis thinks about other things, too—far-away things—as he crosses the dark mission patio. He sees himself back home in South Carolina; sees his angular six-foot body bent over the law books in Judge James Dellet's offices; he sees himself standing before his class, where he teaches school in the mornings so as to be able to study law in the afternoons; a quick pain crosses his heart as he pictures Rosana Cate, a pupil, whose deep blue eyes reflect a vivacity not in keeping with her schoolroom decorum; his frame quivers as he recalls Rosana's young, eager body passionately blending with his . . . their baby son . . . the family doctor tapping his chest, telling him he must seek a dry climate—if he is to live . . . his parting from Rosana, her warm, affectionate letters telling about a new child, a baby girl born after his departure . . . the coolness that crept into her letters, her demands for divorce . . . his anguish and helplessness; his joining the Texas struggle for independence . . . his wild, reckless gambles with his life.

Ah, *his life!* Lungs consumed with fever and heart beating coldly. The Alamo and exhilaration . . . the blood of the slain Mexican is in his nostrils, and buoyed by an acute sense of momentary supremacy and a vague unreasoning craving to meet death, Travis is impatient for the battle to begin. He recalls the letter he had dispatched to General Houston: ". . . I am besieged by four thousand Mexicans under General Santa Anna. . . . *I shall never surrender or retreat.* . . . I am determined to sustain myself as long as possible and die like a soldier who never forgets what is due his own honor and that of his country. *Victory or Death!*"

2:46 A.M.

Colonel James Bowie raises himself on one elbow. He studies Travis's face. At the foot of Bowie's cot sits Big Sam, Bowie's faithful Negro servant, and in a remote part of the room on a pallet of Indian blankets is a young woman. In her arms she enfolds a child. Sam and the woman look anxiously at Travis. Nobody speaks. Finally, from Travis: "Jim, you all right? No pain?"

Bowie ignores the solicitude about his health. "When, Bill?" he asks, fixing the young officer with his steady, slate-gray eyes.

"About daybreak, I figure."

The woman gives a little gasp. Bowie and Travis turn and face her. Her eyes are like a frightened doe's. She raises her face to them, imploring. In a kindly voice Colonel Travis speaks to her. "Mrs. Dickenson, would you like me to send in your husband?"

The woman chokes on words but nods her gratitude.

"They'll hit us with all they've got"—Travis to Bowie. "And it'll be to the tune of the *degüello*. But by God, Jim, it'll cost Santa Anna!"

"Any regrets, Bill?"

"For myself, no."

"I mean," Bowie says slowly, "for not pulling out and blowing up the place."

"Why do you say that, Jim?"

"You know damn well why. Thrice General Houston has ordered us to pull out of here. We're supposed to fall back and join the forces at Goliad. I reckon that General Sam figures we can't hold the Alamo."

"Jim, I joined the Texan revolution to fight, not to run." Travis, his eyes burning, becomes grim. "Dying is part of it."

Bowie looks at the young zealot, a sardonic grin comes hard on his lips. "You *want* to die, damn you! You want to die here in the Alamo. But will dying help General Sam win Texas? First he's got to destroy Santa Anna's forces—and he needs every fightin' man— alive!"

"My mind's made up, Jim. We stay in the Alamo."

"If we don't die here"—Bowie's voice is charged with irony— "we'll all be court-martialed."

"And rightly so—in General Houston's book." Travis grins savagely, a strange light in his eyes. "But I'm not so sure that dying here isn't the best way to destroy Santa Anna."

Bowie challenges Travis with his eyes. "You're crazy and I'm incapacitated. I don't know which is worse for Texas. I'm no more afraid of dying than you are, by God!"

"I'm sure you're not afraid of death, Jim." Travis grins down at Bowie. "But you mightily hate dying."

"Meaning what?" Bowie is caught off guard.

"Jim, are you here because you love Texas? Or are you here— really—to protect all that land you've been paying ten cents an acre for? How many thousand acres have you bought up by now? Santa Anna can disenfranchise you any moment he decrees. It *is* Mexican territory and you are an insurgent . . ." A sly smile crosses Travis's face. "Then you'd never be able to locate the San

Saba mines you've been looking for, on that land you bought at ten cents an acre."

Bowie grins sheepishly. "Bill, you're taking advantage of me. That kind of talk triggered a god-awful brawl between you and me in the Bexar tavern a fortnight ago, as you damn well recall. If I were on my feet I'd whip hell out of you!"

"I'm sure you'd try, Jim. It was a fine fight, and I'm sorry there won't be more of them . . ."

"In that case I'll promise you one thing, by God. I'll waylay you in some dark corner of hell and give you the whippin' you never got in this life!"

"We've got a date, Jim Bowie. Now, down to business. What about the men? Who can we count on? What about Davy Crockett?"

"The Tennessee congressman? I hear he couldn't read or write when they sent him to Washington."

"Maybe so. But he learned fast, real fast. I'm glad he's here. Crockett and his long rifle are worth fifty men. I wonder what brought him out here to Texas?"

Bowie laughs. "A two-barrel dream. He wants to become a war hero. And he wants to kick Andy Jackson you-know-where. That is, after he becomes president of the United States. In Congress he opposed President Jackson's policies, and you can guess how Old Hickory took that. And that speaking tour of the east he made after Congress recessed last term, when the crowds, especially the young folks, mobbed him with adulation—him and his crazy coon cap—that gave Davey a real hankerin' after bear honey. He craves to be a war hero, like Andy Jackson was, then get elected president.—You know he got beat for reelection to Congress."

Bowie laughs, then enjoys a long chuckle. "Yeah. Know how he ended his final speech? I guess he felt he was beat. He said: 'Now, fellow citizens, if you re-elect me, I will serve you to the best of my ability and feel myself always under lasting obligation to you. If you do not elect me you may go to hell and I'll go to Texas!' "

Travis grins. "Think he'll ever make it to the White House?"

"If there was any chance of our beating Santa Anna and winning Texas, he might."

Travis's eyes light up, they burn brightly. "By the saints, Jim! We're going to try!"

Bowie is silent; the silence falls heavily over the dungeonlike little cubicle; the dank adobe-sand smell penetrates the occupants' nostrils. The child in the child-mother's arms whimpers. (Mrs. Dickenson is little more than sixteen years old.)

"What are we? Who are we?" Bowie explodes. "Buccaneers, plunderers, renegades running from the law and from ourselves, entrepreneurs, demagogues? Or are we patriots? You, Bill, damn you, have got some kind of death notion. You came to Texas seeking the arms of death. Of the whole sorry lot of us, General Houston—and maybe Colonel Fannin and one or two others—are the only true patriots. The most of us are, like I said—thieves and murderers running away from ourselves."

"Remember one thing, Jim. No matter what a man falls to, he's always capable of nobility. Maybe we'll find it here in the Alamo."

"Well, no matter what we all are, there's one common denominator: We're all fighters! Yes, Bill, the men will surely fight for you. You'll find your nobility maybe. You'll go to hell in a blaze of glory. And if General Sam can somehow win, monuments will one day be raised in this land bearing your name." Bowie laughs bawdily. "Won't that be one hell of a cynical joke on the politicians and schoolteachers and little children of this land. You know something, Bill. I almost hope that General Sam don't win. Let the truth about us lie buried here with our cursed and damned bones!" Bowie looks at Travis. "You sure you want to take all these men with you, Bill?"

Travis's face softens. "I'll call them together and give them a choice." He turns toward the child-wife in the corner, gives her an affectionate (it was intended to be an encouraging smile), salutes her handsomely. "Ma'am, I'll send someone to escort you to the sacristy. You'll be safer there." He strides out.

"Sam!" Bowie's voice is loud and firm; he is grinning and his fever-ridden eyes glint like anthracite. "Go and fetch two of my boys. Two boys big enough to carry this cot outside!"

3:14 A.M.

Colonel Travis stands before the men of the Alamo. The yellow moon casts a murky light over the scene. The men face their youthful commander in various postures and in all manner of nondescript attire. They wear buckskin breeches and jackets, buffalo hide, wool and fur mackinaws, "beegum" hats, fur headpieces of all descriptions; some are resting on their muskets, some fingering their pistols, others running their thumbs along the edge of their bowie knives.

Without the formality of calling the men to attention, Colonel Travis says what he has to say and gets it over with. "Men"—the level of his voice is friendly but authoritative—"Santa Anna will attack within the hour. We stand one hundred and eighty-three against four thousand. Only a fool would promise you victory. I promise you one thing only—a dear price for the Alamo!" He pauses while with his sword he draws a line between himself and the men. "Any of you who desire to run for it may do so without prejudice. Those wishing to remain and fight kindly step across this line."

Above the rising murmur Bowie's voice is heard. "Boys, set my cot across that line!"

All of Bowie's volunteers instantly follow their leader as he is carried over to Colonel Travis. For the remainder there is a moment of indecision, scraping of feet and mumbling of voices. Then, led by Major James B. Bonham, Travis's friend and aide from South Carolina, one by one and two by two the others cross the line— until but a single man remains on the other side.

He is Moses Rose. He stands there in fur cap, mackinaw and gray cloth trousers. He has no musket, but a horse pistol is thrust between his belt and belly. "Colonel," he says when silence falls over the group. "I am neither a soldier nor a Texan. And I am not a member of the Volunteer Aid. I am a trader, a French trader from Louisiana. I was caught here when the Mexicans marched into San Antonio de Bexar . . ." He falls silent, cut short by the hard stares.

Travis's voice breaks the tension. "Several couriers in the last days have succeeded in penetrating the Mexican lines. It is your privilege to try, Monsieur Rose. You will receive every assistance from these works."

3:39 A.M.

"Sam."

"Yes, Massa James."

"Get some sleep," Bowie says to his faithful servant. "Do you no good to think."

But Jim Bowie does not sleep. He lies on his cot, eyes wide

open, staring at the gray ceiling through the gloom, silently curs-
ing the fates for his incapacity. His lungs are tightening and his
head is on fire. Lieutenant Almaron Dickenson comes into the
room. He kisses his wife and takes his daughter in his arms. The
child awakes, murmurs "Daddy," and, closing her eyes, falls almost
instantly asleep again with a tiny fist on her daddy's cheek.

In a choked, hardly audible voice, Susanna Dickenson asks,
"What will happen?"

"I'm taking you to a safer place." Her husband's voice is urgent.
"No matter what happens, don't go into the yard. I cannot be with
you. Sue . . . my darling!"

She clings to him. A sob breaks from her lips. "Oh, Al! . . ."

Their voices fall on James Bowie's ears but he does not hear
them. He is listening to other voices. "Jamie, my darling . . ." The
vision of Ursula, his wife—his life—hovers before his feverish eyes,
her dark liquid eyes overflowing with love for him. The moment
Juan Martin Veramondi, vice-governor of the Mexican state of
Tejas, introduced him to his slender eighteen-year-old daughter
with the light olive skin, Jim Bowie knew that at last he was in
love. And for her he had become a Mexican citizen. So little time,
it seemed, they have had together. "But Jamie," she said when he
was leaving, "must you go away again!" The last good-bye was
the most painful. He was sending her south to Moncolova to escape
the danger of the yellow plague—the *vomito*, as the Mexicans called
it. She had clung to him tenderly. With the strange mysterious
foreboding of a woman deeply in love she had fought against this
parting. "Jamie, my darling, please! Please, come with me!" But
he had sent her alone and it was too late; already the yellow fumes
of death were coursing through her veins.

How many times during these days of waiting had he climbed
the circular staircase to the bell tower of the mission and, gazing
at the white walls of the town, thought of the happy days he had
known there. Once more, for a little while, he would have Ursula
at his side, hear the musical ring of her laughter, feel the touch of
her hand upon his cheek. Then he would put the vision away,
climb down the tower, thankful that in the action of this revolutionary movement he could find some surcease from his loneliness.
It was Bowie who had run up the Mexican Constitutional flag of
1824 on the Alamo. This was the rightful flag. General Santa Anna,
with the army supporting him, and with an egotistical mania to

emulate Napoleon in the Western world, had usurped the government of Mexico and made himself dictator.

Lying helpless on his cot there in the darkness of the Alamo chapel, Jim Bowie swears silently. Were he capable of tears he could shed them now. Not out of self-pity, but out of cold fury at being unable to stand up and die fighting. James Bowie, the most feared and respected fighter of the century—dying of natural causes! James Bowie, in whose name schools of knife-fighting had sprung up all over the Southwest. Although it was he who had brought undying fame to the Bowie knife, it was his brother Rezin who had designed the blade and Noah Smithwick who had manufactured it. "With this knife, Jim," Rezin had told him, "you can cut both ways. As you can see, several inches of its point end is sharpened on both edges."

He had not long to wait to put it to the crucial test. Returning home to Texas, he was set upon by three desperados hired for the express purpose of killing him. Bowie drew his new knife and with a single stroke of its fifteen-inch blade cut off the first assassin's head. One of the others stabbed him in the leg. He leaped from his saddle, swung his knife upward, disemboweling his second victim. The man, dropping his knife and trying to stay his entrails which were cauliflowering out of his belly, looked up at Bowie with fright and hatred. "Goddamn you, Bowie, you've killed me!" The third man attempted to run away but Bowie caught up with him and split his skull to the shoulders. The blade that his brother had invented was a most terrible weapon.

Thinking, thinking, the long trail—forty years of wonderful, exciting ribbon of life he has trailed behind him, leaving a colorful and fascinating pattern. A surge of deep affection rises in Bowie as he thinks of the brave men who will die with him here. Yes, brave and fearless men; but are not rebels and outlaws always brave and fearless men? Here are men from many states and several nations. Jim Bonham of South Carolina, Bob McKinney of Tennessee, Isaac White of Louisiana, Dan Cloud of Kentucky, Bill Johnston of Philadelphia, Will Lightfoot of Virginia, Tom Jackson of Tennessee, Jose Maria Guerrero of Laredo, Charley Nelson of Charleston, John Garvin of Missouri, and Gregorio Esparza of San Antonio de Bexar; and there is Robert Ballantine from Scotland, Jim Durkin from England, Chuck Hawkins from Ireland, Charley Zanco from Denmark; men from many places, men with roots and hearts in faraway lands. Men with eyes for the space beyond the plain and a hunger for the land behind the mountain. These mortal men, who for thirteen days have left their offal on the ground in the cattle pen in the southeast corner of the mission grounds or buried it in shallow graves beside their sleeping pads, would soon meet their last enemy, death, and then would lie alike upon the ground or in shallow graves, their bodies stilled by the cessation of life, to join in stench and decay their feculence. For the first time in his life Jim Bowie is sorry he cannot cry. Suddenly there is the sweet taste of life in his nostrils. From deep in his memory come poetic words, heard long ago from the lips of his religious mother: "Life, like a dome of many-colored glass, stains the white radiance of Eternity, until death tramples it to fragments." Lying there in the gloom he wishes with all his might to shed tears for these gusty volunteers, who were willing to die for what David Crockett's Tennesseans like to call "our rights." David Crockett! There is a man!

David Crockett had been called "The Indian Fighter." But in truth he was a sincere friend of the Indians. Hadn't he led the fight in Congress against his friend, President Andrew Jackson, on behalf of the Indians? The rough-hewn woodsman from the Reelfoot country in Tennessee had proved in the Congress of the United States to be a man with a high degree of solemnity. Natural ability had supplied what he lacked in education and made of him a man of power and cunning. If Bowie was popular in the Southwest as a fighter and leader of men, Crockett was renown throughout the whole country as a fighter and a politician who thinks of the next generation rather than of the next election. His popularity extended far beyond the regions of his native Tennessee. Whenever he appeared in public places he was met by cheering crowds. His enthusiastic reception far and wide made it clear that this was a man with just the right mixture of color, adventurer, hero, and politician to ride the next political crest in young America. "Old Hickory," whose keen political acumen told him grudgingly that America was not ready for David Crockett on a horse and that David Crockett was not the man for such a mount. This had a lot to do with Crockett's being in Texas. Andy Jackson, nursing his malaria at The Hermitage down in Tennessee, had called in the local political hatchets and passed the word, "Cut the coonskin cap down to size." David Crockett was defeated and left for Texas.

3:45 A.M.

In the yard Colonel Travis, Major Bonham, and Lieutenant Dickenson are busy stationing the men, distributing powder, ball and lighting fuses. Travis is especially attentive to the cannon, since he himself will command the artillery. Save for the two four-pounders guarding the low eight-foot wall and three twelve-pounders put in position on an earthen mound extending to the level of the chapel's east roof, the remainder of the cannon are mounted on the roof of the chapel itself. The little force at the Alamo is numerically unable to man the entire wall adequately, but with the cannon thus positioned Travis will be able to rake the enemy on all sides. The main powder supply for all arms, that used for the riflemen as well as that of the cannoneers, he orders brought and stored in the chapel.

Crockett and his twelve loyal Tennesseans have taken their position on the eight-foot outer wall. Crockett, standing, is ramming a charge down the barrel of his musket. Every day since the beginning of the siege the figure of this man, his coon cap covering his red head, could be seen on the wall firing his long rifle, and coolly standing there to reload. He has become a familiar tableau to the Mexicans. They have learned to stay out of range of his deadly far-firing gun. They know his name is Crockett and that he calls his gun "Betsy." Corrupting and compounding the two, they refer to him as "Kroketsy." Travis inspects the little force of Tennesseans, is quite satisfied, gives Crockett a cheery salutation. He has nothing to say to these men. Each knows what to do: kill Mexicans.

3:50 A.M.

Two men sit on their haunches at the foot of the wall, their Kentucky rifles across their laps. Through the night shadows they can see the outline of each other's faces, bewhiskered and unwashed. Both are wearing buckskin and homespun. "Ole Mose shore wuz a-goin' across that prairie, warn't he?"

The other man chuckles. "He shore wuz! I declare, I never seen a man so anxious to git to New Orleans. Reckon he'll get there?"

"I reckon he will, at thet. When we let 'im down th' wall on thet blanket and the Mex didn't get 'im right then and thar, I figured he had a chanct."

"He shore wuz lucky. They'd shore carve 'im up if'n they'd ketch 'im. But I reckon he got away, all right."

The two fall silent. From over the wall floats the sound of clomping sandals and the scraping and creaking of equipment being moved into position, the low rumble of Spanish. "Ira . . . I been thinkin' . . ."

"Wa'al don't. Here, Ben, have a chaw o' terbaccer."

"We cain't beat the Mex this time, can we, Ira?"

"Naw, but we shore can kill a passel of 'em."

3:52 A.M.

General Antonio Lopez Santa Anna, president and dictator of the Republic of Mexico, sits in his marquee. He is surrounded by aides and lieutenants who are moving about like automatons at their supreme commander's bidding. The furnishings surrounding the president-general are elegant: silver teapots and cream pitchers, monogrammed china, crystal tumblers and decanters with gold stoppers.

In the dimly lighted rear of the tent, sitting in the middle of his large bed with feet drawn up under her as children are wont to do, is Leota. Completely nude, childlike, she is unashamed and unabashed. In Santa Anna's presence she has learned to disrobe discreetly and casually. It is his desire to see her nude, sitting in the center of his bed, awaiting his pleasure. And at the most unexpected moments he will throw himself lovingly upon her. Sometimes he will approach her and sink his hard fingers into the soft flesh of the inside of her thighs, kiss her body, bite her lips until they bleed, then, shudderingly, gently caress her bosom and suddenly turn away from her with a beatific smile on his lips. All this the girl tolerates with a vague, sweet devotion, always submissive and with serene compliancy. Whenever her lord is not present she quickly slips into one of the silken robes or costumes which the great man has showered upon his new toy. Conferences with his aides are usually held in the forepart of the marquee. Whenever his voice rises, Leota lifts her big soft eyes and glances tenderly in his direction.

Seven days ago Leota was but a child playing in her mother's patio in San Antonio de Bexar. When this "god," bedecked in glittering gold braid and bright uniform, rode into the town at the head of his column amid the waving of banners and the trumpeting of lively airs and the stirring Te Deum, his eyes had fallen on Leota; the girl was amid the curious, admiring crowd, holding on to her mother's hand. The next day he had made her his "wife" by means of a fake marriage, to satisfy her religious mother. Now she is "Dona"—at the age of thirteen! From the shadows of the marquee she looks with adoration (or is it gratitude?) upon her lord's expressive countenance, his dark, fine eyes, his rampant black pompadour, his thick, almost negroid lips, his pallor, his melancholy air—"placid madness" her mother had called it with simple admiration.

When the massacre of the Alamo is over, this child will be sent in Santa Anna's private coach, alone and lonely, back to Mexico to be ensconced in a house on one of the dictator's estates (near the city of Jalapa), to be ever at his beck and call. How many others like her there will be Leota will never know. But her life will be quite content, far away from San Antonio de Bexar and her mother, in a strange land. Santa Anna, by no means a mystic, believes as did his historical hero, Napoleon, that a successful military campaign is not quite possible without the blessings of a young maiden's love for the general. Leota is not her true name. But Santa Anna liked the sound and it "seems so perfect for this little flower," he had said after the bogus ceremony.

Santa Anna, reading a pamphlet, suddenly trembles with fury. It is a pamphlet labeled *Santa Anna's Dictionary,* a sample of the surreptitious literature that is being distributed in Mexico by those the general-dictator has suppressed. He reads: "Army: a collection of automatons which are moved like pieces on a chessboard at the will of the player. When they lack bread give them false finery and they are contented. When they become uneasy discipline them and they are silent." "Patriotism: the art of deceiving the public by giving them false facts." "Oath: a ridiculous formula which I am accustomed to go through with and which I break daily." "Patria: a large area of land which I am able to dispose of at pleasure as of my own house." "Mexicans: poor devils whom I have deceived whenever it suits me and whom I control by kicks."

He casts the booklet down. "Where did you get this, General Almonte?"

"I found it in the hands of one of your officers, sir."

"Bring him to me!"

The officer is brought before Santa Anna. He is a cavalry captain and wears the silver cross of the Legion of Honor, a special decoration Santa Anna has created for those who serve in the Texas campaign.

"Captain, have you been circulating this trash among the soldiers?"

"I took it from an infantryman this morning, *mi General estimado.* I do not know his name, nor can I identify him, sir."

"Captain, I regret that you shall not be with me when I plant the Mexican flag in Washington. *Adios!*" To Almonte: "Have this man shot!"

The officer is whisked away. Santa Anna addresses his staff. "The attack shall begin."

"*Muy estimado General,* may I say something?"

"Speak, General Almonte."

"It will cost much."

Santa Anna rises, reaching for his gold-braided and plumed hat. "It is of no importance what the cost may be. It must be done." He places the ornate hat on his head, takes from his desk drawer a small bottle, pries the cork stopper from the bottle's mouth with a penknife, carefully measures a small portion of the snow-white contents on the knife's blade, places it on his tongue, then washes it down with a sip of water. He places the stopper back in the bottle, which is labeled "Sulphate of Morphine," over which is stamped a skull and crossbones in red printing. Santa Anna takes his stand before his marquee: one leg straight and rigid, the other slightly forward, right hand thrust inside his tunic grasping his left breast, glances toward San Fernando Cathedral. "General Almonte, when I fire a blunderbuss from yon church, sound the bugles!"

4:03 A.M.

The assassin-wild notes of the *degüello* rise, slowly and ominously at first, then fill the air from all sides, crescendoing fiercely. The barbaric call mingles with the terrible yells and screams of *Los Zapadores* and the deafening WHAM—WHAM—WHAM! of the muskets, the BAA—ROMMMMMM—BAA—ROMMM! of the cannon, and the PONGG—PONGG—BEE—ZZZING! of pistol shots.

"Here they come, boys!" David Crockett yells from the wall. He is looking down the length of his Betsy rifle, calm and relaxed. His eyes, as they focus the gun sight between the eyes of a charging, screaming Mexican, take in the lettering imprinted into the steel of Betsy just behind the lockplate: *N. Shennefelt—Clarion, Pa.* He squeezes the trigger. The Mexican stumbles forward, his carbine slipping from his hands. On they come, the dark mass of men, across the plain, little spurts of flame, red and yellow, licking out of their muskets. The sullen roar of Travis's cannon atop the chapel, shattering the night, belch grape and cannister, cutting them down. Yet on they come, wave after wave, the cannon and the deadly fire from the wall taking a terrible toll.

Los Zapadores scurry up the ladders, yelling and firing. "Cut 'em down, men!" The Tennessee stalwarts fire their muskets, discharge their pistols, club them back. Ladders are thrown from the wall. Mexicans fall, screaming, from the rungs. No time at close range to reload, the Tennesseans smash skulls with the barrels and butts of their guns, they split heads and hack off arms with their knives. Crockett is standing on the wall. He swings his rifle by the barrel, laying out Mexicans; they fall, brained, in all directions. "Knock their heads off, boys! Roll 'em back!"

4:13 A.M.

Travis, his eyes burning like firebrands, is all over the roof at once, catlike, excited, exhilarated. The cannoneers are inspired by his fire and zeal. They work like demons. Brandishing his sword, he spurs them on. BAA–ROMMM! Flame, thunder and lead spit from the cannon. Another fuse is lowered to the firing plate, another cannon lurches, belches flame and death, rolls back. "At it, men! Fuses!" BAA–ROMMM! Again. Again. "Steady with the big one, boys! Aim 'er! Touch 'er off!" BAA–ROMMM! "More fuses, more powder, more balls!" "Never mind the heat, boys!" "Reload!" "Fire!" Thick smoke hangs over everything. The acrid sulphur-based gunpowder fumes smarts the eyes and chokes the lungs. Travis is overtaken with a fine, excited sense of well-being. His cannon are doing effective work. The Mexican lines are mercilessly raked, are being blasted back. His cannon are killing, killing, killing! *"Victory or Death!"*

4:21 A.M.

The attack on Crockett's sector having been repulsed, the Mexicans mount an assault on the sixteen-foot south wall, where a company of cavalry under Lieutenant Dickenson are stationed on a plank platform adjacent to the wall. The Mexicans hoist their ladders, scurry up like frenzied rats. Santa Anna's cavalry is driving the fleeing Mexicans onto the wall. With the unreasoning fury of madmen they are wild to get up and over; in their confused imagination they fancy there is safety on the other side. Dickenson's men stand like stout oaks. They wait, a head pops up over the rampart, they blast at close range: a face becomes a powder-burned mass of bloody flesh, torn skull bones, scattered brains. Horrible screams pierce the air. Guns empty, they hack and hammer the Mexicans with swords and sword hilts. It is a victory for Dickenson but a costly one. The platform and ground beneath are covered with dead Americans.

4:29 A.M.

"Where'd he git you, Ira?"

"In the neck. I reckon I ain't gonna do no more Mex killin' today, Ben." Blood has covered his face and is flowing all over his buckskin shirt.

"I'll git you over to th' chapel, Ira."

"Leave me be. Mind out for yerself, Ben . . ."

"Yeah, Ira?"

"Got a chaw o' thet terbaccer?"

"I'll git 'im, Ira! I'll git thet goddamn Mex that got you! I'll git a dozen!" He gives his buddy his plug of tobacco, climbs back up on the wall. Standing high, knife poised, he leaps, spread-eagled and yelling ferociously, down into a mob of milling, stewing Mexicans.

4:55 A.M.

"General! Our *zapadores* are driven back!" It is General Almonte, out of breath.

"Turn them round with the cavalry. Drive the cowards back to the wall."

"But, my *estimado Generaldo*, there's none to turn round!"

"None! What are you saying, Almonte!"

"Out of a thousand *zapadores*, over eight hundred are lying in their blood at the foot of the wall."

Santa Anna paces up and down. His eyes, their brilliance heightened by morphine, are dancing beads of onyx. His face is suffused with cold fury, the raging, frustrating fury that overtakes a man of extreme ego whose ambition is suddenly defeated through weakness or failure of others. "General Almonte! Ready all reserves. Every man! We will hit that wall with everything! This time it will be the ultimate *Malebolge*—the eighth circle of hell for the Americanos! They will find that Santa Anna is more evil than if the devil himself were on that wall!"

5:06 A.M.

While the Mexicans regroup, the little band of Americans inside the battered bastion move their wounded into the barracks and rally the able-bodied men for the next assault. Surgeon Pollard, working alone—Doctors Michison and Thompson are among those killed—moves swiftly among the bleeding and dying, stanching a spurt of blood here, applying a tourniquet there, shaking his head hopelessly over a torn body. Many he sends back to the wall with "Only a scratch, my boy. Load up and get back out there!"

"Fifty-one dead, seventy-eight wounded," Pollard announces to Travis.

"How many of the wounded can still fight?"

"About half."

"Good! Let the Mexicans come! We'll raise the price for Santa Anna!"

5:34 A.M.

The final assault is launched on all sides of the Alamo. The Mexican cannon roar close, hard and steady. The yelling and noise is fiercer and more desperate. Streaks of light, shooting up over the eastern edge of the world, cast an eerie pallor over the little force pitifully scattered along the expanses of the walls. Ninety-three men to defend nearly three acres of enclosure! The Mexicans charge from every direction, frantically driven by their harangued and threatened officers. Cavalry, cannoneers, *zapadores*, officers, clerks, and cooks are climbing upon the walls. Santa Anna will have no more failures.

Travis's cannon scatter and halt them at first—until he has fired his last cannonball. He rams nail, scrap, rock—whatever comes to hand—down the muzzles of the guns. But he cannot discharge these near the walls; he will cut down his own men. He directs his fire at Santa Anna's baggage and rear guard. From his vantage point on the roof he sees, with cold and bitter heart, Mexicans rolling over the walls from all sides.

Crockett and his men are quickly overrun. "Fall back, boys! But slowly, keep facing 'em!" The Tennesseans pistol, club, knife their retreat back toward the barracks. "We'll make a stand inside!" But only Crockett and two stalwarts succeed. The others lie strewn all the way from the wall to the barracks.

5:45 A.M.
Sam, whom Bowie has sent to peek outside, scurries back in. "They're tryin' to git in, Massa James! They're comin' over de walls! What we do now?"

"Nothing, Sam. My pistols! Give them to me. Here . . . prop me up. Now go to Miss Sue and the child."

5:51 A.M.
Crockett and his two remaining Tennesseans have made a last stand in a small room at the end of the barracks hallway. They have fought the Mexicans to a standstill. The Mexicans, wary of dead-shot "Kroketsy," are loath to rush him. "Three pistols, three muskets," Crockett says. "You men get behind me. Load 'em and pass 'em to me."

Outside, a Mexican officer, sword in hand, prods the soldiers into the hallway. A steady lethal fire comes from the end of the hall. Dead Mexicans clutter the floor and jam the hallway. They fall, victims of Crockett's guns. Flattened upon the floor and firing from the narrow doorway, Crockett is not an easy target. The Mexican officer realizes he must take a drastic measure to put an end to the terrible massacre. He orders his men out of the hallway. There is a small conference, a respite, the noises of the soldiers clearing out their dead. Silence, save for the Mexicans roaming through the other rooms and killing the wounded on their cots.

Crockett hears an infuriating exchange of words from one of the rooms. "Don't kill me! Here—see—I have money. Good American money. I give to you! Here, take it. Spare my life."

Si, Señor. You got money. What else you got?"

"My watch! Here, take it. You won't kill me, will you? Listen! I'm David Crockett. Understand? David Crockett! You are a brave soldier. I'm brave fighter, too. You don't want to kill David Crockett. I'm a Congressman of the United States!"

"This all you got, Señor? Money and watch?"

"That's all . . . . ."

BLOOWAMM!

Comes the sound of heavy steel on stone floor. The Mexicans

are dragging a cannon down the hallway. The cannon's muzzle is shoved into the room and instantly it belches fire, smoke, and an inordinate charge of grape, wreaking terrific havoc. Crockett's right arm is blown off; his two companions are killed instantly. Crockett takes his knife in his remaining hand. Trailing strings of blood thickened with pulverized flesh and bone from the stub of his splintered arm, he moves to the center of the room. "I'm still here! Come in and get me! *I'm David Crockett!*"

Driven by their officers, a group of Mexicans charge down the hallway, howling savagely and shooting indiscriminately. David Crockett, the Tennessean who might have been President, steps out to meet them. Ball after ball tears through his body. On he comes toward his executioners. Another volley. He stumbles, knife in hand. Rifle butts come down upon his head, breaking bone. Again. Again. Again. . . .

5:57 A.M.

Mexicans are everywhere, swarming over the yard. They go from body to body, bayonetting, hacking, mutilating the wounded and dead alike. It is a barbaric, incontinent feast of blood. Was this victory? How seldom has such a sweetness come to the Mexican army!

Travis hails Lieutenant Dickenson from the top of the chapel. "Here!" he shouts, throwing Dickenson a lighted fuse. "Blow up the chapel! The powder magazine—inside!"

Dickenson hesitates. "That's an order!" Travis shouts. Dickenson stands there, frozen between duty to his commanding officer and love of his wife and baby, the lighted fuse sputtering in his hand. Travis, his eyes like two marbles of glowing slag in the pit of a furnace, draws his pistol, cocks it, puts it to his temple and fires. His body slumps across a cannon. Dickenson, seeing a dozen Mexicans charging him, carbines drawn, dashes into the doorway of the chapel. He will carry out Travis's last command. Multiple shots ring out behind him; he drops in the doorway of the sacristy. The fuse in his hand falls to the floor, burns brightly, then blinks out, trailing a little feather of white smoke ceilingward.

The Mexicans tramp over Dickenson's body, bayonetting and hacking, squeeze into the room where Bowie has propped himself up on his cot, a pistol in each hand. He squeezes both triggers simultaneously. One arm jerks back with the impact, the other pistol misfires. He throws them at the Mexicans, draws his knife.

"Here, Jim, take old Bowie. She'll never snap," he hears his brother Rezin's voice.

A dozen bayonets converge upon him, and he hears other voices.

"Goddamn you, Bowie, you've killed me!" And still another voice, softer, warm and musical. "But Jamie, it seems that you are always going away . . ."

6:30 A.M.

A bright Texas sun bathes the Alamo courtyard in warm light. A profound quiet lies over everything. Only the drip, drip, drip of blood can be heard. A cock crows mournfully in the distance. Half a mile away at the chapel of Mission Concepcion several old women from San Antonio de Bexar are kneeling and offering up prayers for the dead, Mexicans and Americans. A maiden with Latin skin and solemn eyes comes into the Alamo, searching among the dead. She finds the American who had become her sweetheart. She folds his arms, soaks her handkerchief in his blood and slips away to Sunday morning mass.

Supreme General Santa Anna, accompanied by his staff, inspects the battleground. The stillness is broken by a group of soldiers, now drunk, rushing out of the barracks carrying the body of a big, red-headed man high on their bayonets. "Kroketsy! Kroketsy!" they are crying.

"Kroketsy?" Santa Anna inquires.

"David Crockett," Alamonte explains.

"Yes, Crockett. He's the tall one with the long gun who's been trying to pick me off. Burn them. Make a pyre outside somewhere —anywhere. Burn them all!" Then in a quiet voice: "But gather our own dead and give then a decent burial."

"Very good, sir." Alamonte's voice assumes an apologetic tone. "But there will be two thousand graves . . ."

Entering the chapel, Santa Anna finds Susanna Dickenson cowering in a corner. Old Sam is beside her, holding the child. Santa Anna uncovers the babe's face. "Take them to my marquee," he orders. "See that they are not harmed. I will need someone to take the message to Houston. Texans must know how we deal with rebels!"

Inspecting room after room, with his train of admiring officers close on his heels, Santa Anna points to a mutilated body lying on a blood-soaked cot. "And that?"

"Colonel James Bowie," Alamonte replies.

Santa Anna approaches the cot, gazes silently for a moment, removes his decorative hat to the man who had once been his friend and who had died as his enemy. "He was much too brave a man to be treated like a dog. Bury him with my soldiers." He looks at Alamonte, then thoughtfully at the floor. "Two thousand dead, you say?"

Replacing his plumed hat, Santa Anna strides out. At the doorway he pauses, his last fiber of mercy spent. "It is of little consequence. Burn Bowie with the other rebels."

13
Lest We Forget...

I N closing this study, it is pleasant to turn away from the conflict and cruelty, struggle and violence, and fire and death that we have just witnessed at the Alamo, and return to the Franciscan fathers, whose sublime devotion to the souls of men brought to Texas the hope and enlightenment without which its present level of civilization would not have been possible. All that is noble, good, and beautiful in the life which Texans enjoy today has been achieved for them by men inspired by the grace of God. The record of those glorious achievements are mementos of the perpetual memory of those friars in their brown robes who trudged barefoot through the night and wilderness of Texas and carried the torch of Christian civilization to that inhospitable frontier. They planted the cross in the good earth there and the lance and the sword disappeared from the land; and the ever glowing flame of their torch is a priceless treasure passed on to posterity.

The Franciscan friars are gone, but the culture and philosophy which they implanted have survived and are a force in the lives of all who live in their shadow. They have left us the heritage of their labors of nearly a century and a half, and with it a trust—a trust to preserve and perpetuate that nobility, that beauty, that tolerance and love for one's fellow man, regardless of the color of his skin or the level of his enlightenment, in accordance with the eternal designs of the Creator of mankind.

Those who cherish a Christian faith in the divinity of the human creature must surely believe that each dead hand relinquishes a light, and each living hand carries it on. Those of us existing in today's world of splendor are living proof of the early Franciscan fathers' faith in that divine light within us. They understand this well, and never, for a moment, wavered in their passionate belief

171

in its perseverance. The old missions of Texas stand as monuments to that faith and to the departed love and power of the devoted Little Brothers. Perhaps, then, in times of despair, when we may doubt that love and power, we need but look again upon those monuments and remember not the Alamo or Goliad or San Saba, but Saint Francis of Assisi, who, himself in a moment of dismay, looked for guidance and in a divine revelation heard these words: "Francis, repair my church which falleth into ruins . . ."

Principal Sources

Adair, Anthony Garland, *The Siege of the Alamo*. Jericho, New York: Exposition Press, 1957.

Bolton, Herbert Eugene, *La Expopeya de la Maxima America Mexico DF*. Institute Panamericano de geograffia e historia publicacion: 30, 1937.

—— *Spanish Explorations in the Southwest*. New York: Barnes and Noble, 1938.

—— *Texas in the Middle 18th Century*. Berkeley: University of California Press, 1915.

—— *The Mission as a Frontier Institution in the Spanish American Colonies*. Introduction by John Alexander Carroll. El Paso: Texas Western College Press, 1960.

—— *The Padre on Horseback*. San Francisco: The Sonora Press, 1932.

—— *With the Makers of Texas*. Austin: Gammel Statesmen Publishing Company, 1904.

Brooker, William H., *History of Texas*. Columbus, Ohio: Press of Nitschke Bros., 1897.

Brooks, Charles Mattoo, Jr., *Spanish Missions of Texas*. Dallas: Dealey and Lowe, 1936.

Burke, Thomas J., *Beyond All Horizons*: Jesuit Missions. New York: Hanover House, 1957.

—— *Catholic Mission*. New York: Fordham University Press, 1957.

Burke, William, *Of the Spanish Settlement*. London: J. Dodsley, 1766.

Butterfield, Jack C., *Men of the Alamo, Goliad, and San Jacinto*. San Antonio: 1936.

Casteneda, Carlos Eduardo, *Our Catholic Heritage in Texas*. Vol I (1936), Vol. II (1938), Vol. III (1939), Vol. IV (1939). Austin: Van Baeckman-Jones Company.

173

Chabot, Frederick Charles, *San Fernando*. San Antonio: The Naylor Company, 1930.

—— *The Alamo Mission—Shrine*. San Antonio: The Leake Company, 1935.

—— *The Indians and the Missions*. San Antonio: The Naylor Company, 1935.

—— *With the Makers of San Antonio*. San Antonio: The Naylor Company, 1937.

Clark, Thalia Dubose, *Spanish-Moorish Influence Upon the Troubadour and Europe*. Dallas: Southern Methodist University Press, 1934.

Coggershall, William Turner, *Frontier Life and Character of the Southwest*. Columbus: Folliet, Foster and Company, 1896.

Connell, Will, *Spanish Missions of California*. New York: Hastings House, 1941.

Conner, Seymour V., *The Saga of Texas 1519–1965*. Austin: Steck Vaughn Company, 1965.

Crockett, George Lewis, *Two Centuries in East Texas*. Austin: The Southwest Press, 1932.

Curtis, Albert, *Remember the Alamo*. San Antonio: Klegg Company, 1961.

Daniels, James S., *La Junta de los Rice*. MA thesis, Austin: University of Texas, 1938.

Dobie, Frank, *In the Shadow of History*. Austin: Texas Folklore Society, 1939.

Forrest, Earl Robert, *Spanish Missions of Arizona*. Cleveland: Arthur Clark Company, 1929.

Foulche-Dilbosc, Raymond, *Spanish Missions*. Oxford: The Dolphin Company, 1963.

Gunthrop, Maude Robson, *Spanish Missions of California*. Caldwell, Idaho: The Caxton Printers, Ltd., 1940.

Hackett, Charles Wilson, *Essays in Mexican History*. New York: Doubleday, Doran and Company, Inc., 1935.

—— *Historical Documents Relating to New Mexico, Nueva Vizeya*. Washington: The Carnegie Institute, 1923–37.

—— *Picardo's Treatise on the Limits of Louisiana and Texas*. Austin: University of Texas Press, 1931–1946.

—— *Revolt of the Pueblo Indians of New Mexico and Otermin's Attempted Conquest 1680–82*. Albuquerque: University of New Mexico Press, 1942.

Hammer, Laura Vernon, *Frontier and Pioneer Life—Texas*. Norman: University of Oklahoma Press, 1943.

Heusinger, Eduard W., *Early Explorations and Mission Establishments in Texas*. San Antonio: The Naylor Company, 1936.

Hughes, Dorothy B., *Pueblo on the Mesa*. Albuquerque: University of New Mexico Press, 1939.

Kemp, Lewis W., *Burial Place of the Alamo Heroes*. MA thesis, Dallas: Southern Methodist University, 1890.

Kubler, George, *Spanish Missions of New Mexico*. El Paso: Rio Grande Press, 1962.

Lamming, John Tate, *The Spanish Missions of Georgia*. Chapel Hill, The University of North Carolina Press, 1935.

Lord, Walter, *A Time to Stand*. New York: Harper, 1961.

Madlen, Richard Henry, *San Jose Mission*. Oxford: Oxford University Press, 1933.

Marfi, Fray Juan Agustin, Ed., *History of Texas, 1673–1779*. Albuquerque: The Quivira Society, 1935.

McCaleb, Walter Flavius, *Spanish Missions of Texas*. San Antonio: The Naylor Company, 1954.

——— *Texas Missions, Their Romance and Architecture*. Published by author, 1936.

Myers, John M., *The Alamo*. New York: E. P. Dutton, 1948.

Nathan, Paul D., *The San Saba Papers*. San Francisco: J. Howell Books, 1959.

Nixon, Patrick Ireland, *A Century of Medicine in San Antonio*. San Antonio: San Antonio Press, 1936.

Norton, Paul D., Translator, *The San Saba Papers*. San Francisco: John Howell Books, 1953.

Oberst, William H., *Our Lady Comes to Refugio*. Refugio: The Jones Publishing Company, 1944.

——— *History of Refugio Mission*. Refugio: The Jones Publishing Company, 1946.

Payne, Albert Bigelow, *Frontier and Pioneer Life in Texas*. New York: J. J. Little and Ives, 1909.

Pereyra, Carlos, *Historia de America Espanola*. Washington: Library of Congress, 1926.

——— *Texas, First Dismemberment of Mexico*. MA thesis, Dallas: Southern Methodist University, 1918.

Ramsdell, Charles, *San Antonio*. Austin: University of Texas Press, 1968.

Robles, Antonio, *Merry Tales from Spain*. Philadelphia: John C. Winston Company, 1939.

Ryan, William M., *Shamrock and Cactus*. San Antonio: Southern Literary Institute, 1936.

Santa Anna, General, *The Mexican Side of the Revolution*. Dallas: P. L. Turner Company, 1928.

Schuetz, Mardity K., *The Historic Background of Mission San Antonio de Valero*. Austin: Archeological Commission Report Number 1, 1943.

Schwetz, Edward Muegge, *Spanish Missions of Texas—Views*. Austin: University of Texas Press, 1968.

Shea, John Dawson Gilmary, *History of the Missions Among the Catholic Church in California*. New York: P. J. Kennedy Company, 1933.

——— *The Catholic Church in Colonial Days*. Published by the author, 1956.

——— *The Indian Tribes of the USA*. Published by the author, 1956.

Six Missions of Texas. Illustrated by Lon Tinkle, J. B. Frantz, J. W. Schintz, D. H. Winfrey, J. M. Day, and B. Procter. Waco: The Texian Press, 1965.

Southwest Review, Vol. XIII, XIV, Austin: 1963.

Taylor, Henry Ryder, *Alamo*. San Antonio: N. Tengg, 1936.

Taylor, Paul Schuster, *A Spanish-American Peasant Community*. Berkeley: University of California Press, 1933.

Tinkle, Lon, *13 Days to Glory*. New York: McGraw Hill, 1958.

Tolbert, Frank X., *An Informal History of Texas*. New York: Harper Bros. Publishers, 1961.

Weddle, Robert S., *San Saba Mission*. Austin: University of Texas Press, 1964.

Wright, Ione W., *Our Living Alamo*. Dallas: B. Upshaw and Company, 1937.

Yoakum, Henderson K., *A Comprehensive History of Texas*. Austin: The Steck Company, 1930.

——— *History of Texas from its First Settlement in 1685*. Austin: The Steck Company, 1935.

Zavala, Adina de, *History and Legends of the Alamo and Other Missions in and around San Antonio*. Published by the author, San Antonio, 1917.

Index

177